The Challenges of Modern Sport
to Ethics

The Challenges of Modern Sport to Ethics

From Doping to Cyborgs

José Luis Pérez Triviño

Translated by Julie Scales

LEXINGTON BOOKS
Lanham • Boulder • New York • Toronto • Plymouth, UK

Published by Lexington Books
A wholly owned subsidiary of The Rowman & Littlefield Publishing Group, Inc.
4501 Forbes Boulevard, Suite 200, Lanham, Maryland 20706
www.rowman.com

10 Thornbury Road, Plymouth PL6 7PP, United Kingdom

British Library Cataloguing in Publication Information Available

Library of Congress Cataloging-in-Publication Data

Library of Congress Cataloging-in-Publication Data Available

ISBN Cloth: 978-0-7391-7998-7 (cloth : alk. paper)

Printed in the United States of America

Contents

Acknowledgements

This book is one of the results of a research grant from the Spanish Ministry of Education that allowed me to work for six months at the Oxford Uehiro Center for Practical Ethics (Faculty of Philosophy, University of Oxford), directed by Julian Savulescu to whom I wish to express my deepest gratitude. I also want to mention several colleagues: Alberto Carrio, José Manuel Ríos, David Felip, Enrique Bonete, Blanca Rodríguez, José Antonio Seoane, Francisco Javier López Frías, Fernando Llano, Josep Maria Carbonell and the members of the Philosophy of Law Department of Pompeu Fabra University. Also I would like to thank audiences at the universities of Alicante, Complutense, Cádiz and A Coruña.

My gratitude goes to Claudio Tamburrini for his support and insistence on translating this book. To César Torres for his invaluable friendship. I am especially grateful to Jorge Malem for his personal support and his invaluable comments. In the final stretch, I appreciated Antonio Pérez, my friend and relentless editor of form and content. I do not want to forget to mention my parents and siblings, and neither Ana and Víctor, without whom nothing would be the same at all.

Translation: Julie Scales

Introduction

Everything I know about morality and the obligations of men, I have
learned from football. — A. Camus

The concept of ethical concerns within the field of sport has sprung up
relatively recently, and although this concept has seen great development
until current times, moral reflections about the body and the activities
that we generically call games or athletic tasks can be found in writings
from ancient or modern times. Seldom do those reflections look kindly on
physical activities. Take for example Platonic and Cartesian dualism. For
Plato, the soul must struggle with the demands and passions of the body
in order to finally attain harmony, moderation and awareness. In a similar way, Descartes made a precise distinction between the body and the
mind. Even though both entities were connected at some point through a
problematic union, they were different from each other with the physical
body having an inferior range. This point of view has survived through
current times. In spite of the relevance of sport and the virtues associated
with it in current society, particularly the relationship between health
and personality development, sport in general continues to be seen as an
activity that is not related to reasoning and is, therefore, inferior. Additionally, another recurring theme in relation to sport is that sporting activity engenders further objectionable elements by promoting certain personality traits that are considered negative: competitiveness, aggressive-
ness and nationalism.

But the analysis of ethical questions themselves did not arise until the
twentieth century. This century also witnessed the extremely wide and
varied development of distinct sports which came to be an important
activity in the daily lives of individuals, a money-making business of
enormous dimensions as well as a not insignificant factor of political
cohesion in current societies. In this way, countless hours are devoted to
practicing some sport or to watching it on various media devices. Several
years ago, a report on Americans' attitudes to sports indicated that 96.3
percent of the population plays, watches, or reads articles on sport on a
frequent basis or identifies with a particular team or player (Morgan
2007). In addition, it is well known that at least some disciplines of sport
are "heavy weights" in terms of their economic activity. It suffices to
mention the budgets of football clubs or racing teams, the amount of
money spent on trades, and also the great number of companies devoted
to providing clothing, supplies and accessories for sport. And let us not

1

forget the astronomical prices paid for television broadcast rights. Lastly, the social-political importance that sport plays does not go unnoticed. John Carlin's book *Playing the Enemy: Nelson Mandela and the Game That Changed a Nation* (Carlin 2008) on the role of rugby in the reconciliation between whites and blacks in South Africa provides one of the best examples of the role of sports in this area.

In this book, my aim is to offer an overview of the diverse areas of ethical reflection regarding sport that have developed over the course of recent decades. I am aware that this approach is not exhaustive (for example, I will not analyze the relation between sport and animals, sport and disabilities or matters of meta-ethical character), nor do I intend to offer a static picture of a changing phenomenon. Thus, the objective will be to offer a synthesis of the main ethics-related topics that are found in sport: values (fair play), doping, sport, and violence, sport and matters of sex, and sport and nationalism. Lastly, I will present the main moral challenges that arise in sport through the latest technological developments: gene doping, cyborgs, and the possibility of creating transgenic athletes (hybrids and chimeras). But before analyzing these matters, some conceptual notes are necessary about the phenomenon of sport. This is needed due to the fact that a large part of the philosophical discussion concerning sport has specifically revolved around definitions. In other words, it is important to note the features that distinguish sport from other similar activities: 1) the distinction between play and sport; 2) the role of rules and values in the rule system of sport; and 3) the competitive and recreational nature of sport.

PLAY AND SPORT

Limiting of the concept of sport can be done to a large extent by focusing on the notion of play. In his seminal essay "Homo Ludens," Johan Huizinga (Huizinga 1955) began to define the path which would lead to characterizing the nature of play. This characterization can then be used to refine the concept of "sport." According to Huizinga, games make up a basic element in all cultures throughout history. He characterizes play as a phenomenon that does not form part of "daily" life or life "in and of itself." It is rather a voluntary activity that develops at the edge of the sphere of activities that make up work and ordinary life. It is an activity that flees from the sphere of homo faber (Man the Maker) and possesses a tendency of its own: "[P]lay presents itself to us in the first instance: as an intermezzo, an interlude in our daily lives. As regularly recurring relaxation, however, it becomes an accompaniment, the complement, in fact an integral part of life in general. It adorns life, amplifies it and is to that extent a necessity both for the individual—as a life function—and for society by reason of the meaning it contains, its significance, its expressive value and its spiritual and social associations, in short, as a culture function" (Huizinga 1955).

But the debate quickly became heated regarding the difficult task of differentiating "sport" from "play." It was Wittgenstein who pointed out the difficulty in characterizing the term "play" by using precisely this word as an example of the vague nature of linguistic terms (Torres 2000). It is common knowledge known that "play" consists of things like board games, soccer, war games, childhood games, rugby, boxing, juggling, solitary, the lottery, etc. What do all these have in common? The answer, according to Wittgenstein, is not easy because even though certain similarities and some relationships can be found, it is unlikely that there is a feature common to all of them: they are not all fun, not all of them have winners and losers, not all have competition, not all of them are related to skill or luck, etc.

In spite of the semantic hardships alluded to by Wittgenstein, Bernard Suits highlighted the need to analyze the relationship between sport and play. Curiously, Suits laid out the two great alternatives in the characterization of sport based on the notion of play. In his essay "The Elements of Sport" (Suits 1995 [1973]), he claims that sport is a type of play, while in his later essay "Tricky Triad: Games, Play and Sport" (1988) he argues that some sporting practices exist that cannot be integrated into games. Let us examine both alternatives.

In his first treatment of the relationship between game and sport, Suits advocates that the core (but not the only) characteristics of sport are the same ones that games possess. In this way, he concludes that all sports are games, but not all games are sports. He defines games as any activity that proposes achieving a specific state of affairs using the means allowed by the rules, wherein these rules prohibit the most efficient means of reaching the goal of the game in favor of less efficient ways (constitutive rules) and wherein these rules are accepted, the game becomes possible. As long as a sport is assimilated as part of games, its definition includes these four big-picture elements or traits. However, what distinguishes sport from games are these other characteristics: 1) it is a game of skill; 2) specifically, of physical skill; 3) it is an activity that enjoys a large following by those who take part in it; 4) it is an activity that has enjoyed a certain level of institutional stability.

In his latter approach to the relationship between game and sport, Suits revises his initial theses and proposes a distinction between "athletic events" and "athletic games." Among the former, gymnastics, swimming, and skiing can be found, while in the latter soccer, basketball, and baseball, for example, can be seen. The former are characterized by being guided and shaped perfectionist practices; they constitute ideal ways of carrying out the activity and are not greatly influenced by rules that limit the means to be used in this activity. That is, what is relevant is to approach an ideal perfectionist realization. These practices are not games and do not need referees, but rather judges. On the other hand, athletic games are practices governed by rules that establish the most difficult ways to attain sought-after goals in their practice.

The debate about the characterization of sport has been expanding beyond the initial contributions made by Bernard Suits, and has been, in any case, trying to provide a better profile of the defining traits of sport. By way of example, another interesting discussion related to the characterization of sport is its relationship with fairness (Loland 2002), as well as the role played by luck in defining victory (Breivik 2000).

THE ROLE OF RULES AND CONVENTIONS

The discussion about the role of the rules and the conventions in sport makes up another one of the great philosophical controversies that has kept scholars busy over recent decades. Once again, it was Suits (Suits 1995) who provided the foundation for the discussion by maintaining that the formalist focus, in which great emphasis is placed on the importance of written rules created through established procedures, should guide the purpose and sense of sports. That is, previously determined and specified rules of the sport in question convey what counts as a valid move or corrective action within the framework of the practice of sports, whether this move be scoring or committing an infraction. Based on this approach, a significant part of the study of sporting phenomenon has revolved around the distinction between the types of rules valid in sports and their distinct functions (Suits 1988).

But soon, and not without sound arguments, objections regarding this formalist characterization of sport arose. The main critique directed at the formalist focus of sport is that it gives little consideration to the fact that sports have, in addition to the formal rules laid out in their basic rule framework, something that can be called "ethos." The "ethos" of a sport would be the set of empirically identified social conventions that govern the interpretation of codified rules in particular cases. Morgan (2007) maintains that sports (just like games) rest on the existence of constitutive rules which are the ones that define moves as valid in practice. But in the analysis of sports, "ethos" can always be included, and while the primacy of the rules that champion the formalist focus is maintained, these "ethos" are what confer meaning on the practice of the sport.

As has occurred in other social environments (as is the case of Law, where there has also been a debate between formalist and conventionalist theses), recent decades have seen the appearance of a third way that has chosen to defend a conception of sport that goes beyond the written rules and conventions. It alleges the need to appeal to principles and values that are critical in giving meaning to the practice of sport. This conception is called interpretativism and will be the subject of further analysis in the section devoted to strategic intentional fouls.

RECREATIONAL AND COMPETITIVE NATURE

Another one of the topics garnering philosophical debate regarding the nature of sport revolves around the juxtaposition of two elements that are frequently predicted based on the sport: its recreational nature and its competitive nature. As mentioned above, Huizinga highlighted the recreational character of sport as one of its core features. In terms of this characteristic, sport would be an environment where free choice, cooperation and personal effort of the athlete to achieve personal bests are that factors at play. From this standpoint, the connection between the athlete and his or her rival is not adversarial. Rather it can be understood that the other athlete compels the rival to go beyond and find the best in him or herself (Loland 2002). It is from this perspective that some authors highlight the pursuit of excellence as a core feature of sport.

However, this thesis is not unanimously accepted by the experts. In effect, there is another characteristic: competitiveness. Whether this competitiveness stems from the individual or from competition with others, it is for some unquestionably the most important aspect. This is the case concerning elite and professional sport above all. The competitive characteristic of sport is being reinforced due to the way current societies behave, especially Western ones. The individualist and competitive way of life are all the order of the day. One cannot keep from reflecting on sport and how its recreational and cooperative nature has faded away (López 2010). What's more, for some, the practice of sport has stopped having its main goal be pursuit of excellence in the display of physical skills. Rather, external goals are pursued (economic earnings, fame, etc.) and in this way it stops being a proper sport. The choice or preponderance of one of these extreme opposites is important, not only in theory in its characterization of sport, but also in practice. This practical application is important since every one of them constitute different (and sometimes opposing) "ethos" which lead to results being interpreted very differently, as will be seen in the chapter on strategic intentional fouls.

To round out this introduction, I would like to highlight two points: 1) the plan of the book, the analysis of certain ethical questions in sport, primarily concerns elite or professional sport, and not amateur sport; 2) under the heading of "ethics in sport," two topics of descriptive nature and educational nature have developed historically. In the former, the studies have been mainly sociological in nature. In the latter, there were attempts to focus on which virtues sport generates among practitioners and which strategies should be followed in order to foster this transmission of values. However, what is characteristic of this philosophical-moral reflection in recent years has been a systematic conceptual analysis of characteristic terms relating to the sporting phenomenon and the ethical-normative problems. This is the focus that I have followed in this work.

ONE

Moral Value of Sport

Fair Play, Cheating, and Strategic Intentional Fouls

Some people think that football is a question of life or death. It's more important than that. —Bill Shankly, FC Liverpool Manager

The analysis of so-called "strategic intentional fouls," as well as the discussion of their validity in the rule systems of sports, has a long track record. While a more detailed explanation will be provided below, for now it will suffice to mention that these fouls can be characterized as rule violations committed in order to be detected and accept the corresponding sanction. However, there is actually a concurrent goal of obtaining an advantage or subsequent benefit in the competition. In fact, this practice is not infrequent, and it is even accepted by the players themselves, referees, judges, sports authorities, and spectators. An example is the deliberate foul in basketball (e.g., grabbing the rival player who has control of the ball) at the end of a game, taking the free throws in order to interrupt the opposing team's possession and take the shooter inside the three-point line. Another example, quite commonly used in the world of soccer, is known as "self-booking"; here a yellow card is intentionally provoked in order to draw the following red card, thus completing the penalty-card cycle and the resulting suspension from a match against a minor rival. This allows the player to be available for a match that is considered more relevant at a later stage of a tournament.

This discussion is about the moral acceptability of strategic intentional fouls (SIFs), which is not only of interest for the players of sports themselves in the debate on the tactics used in sports; it is also of interest at the philosophical-moral level since accepting these strategies would involve, at least according to some theorists, accepting a strategy that is contrary to the principles and values that are considered part and parcel of sports

7

themselves. Likewise, the acceptance of these fouls would constitute an example of how the emphasis on winning has debased the most profound and fundamental values which make sport a morally attractive business (Simon 2007; 216). In particular, critics fear and suspect that accepting strategic fouls would imply prioritizing a thirst for victory over other valuable characteristics of sport. In effect, for the critics of SIFs, what is relevant about the sport is that it is in its essence a physical test of the competitors' abilities, not the search for triumph or victory over a rival. Only when the comparison of abilities is carried out in line with the structural values of the sport will victory have any meaning. This is not the case if these structural values are infringed upon. A disproportionate emphasis on results and external compensation (e.g., fame and fortune) which go along with victory should not lead participants to lose sight of the integrity of the activity itself.

There is a another discussion concerning whether these fouls contradict the spirit of the game, the conventions or the principles that govern the practice of sport, or rather, if their use can be considered legitimate since using this strategy is not explicitly prohibited by the system of rules governing sports. Additionally, this thinking seems to be accepted in certain sporting disciplines, that is, it is taken as forming part of the game. Some of them are accepted in the conventions (ethos) of the diverse sport practices and others are not considered entirely acceptable; that is to say, it is debatable whether they are recognized by the sport ethos. The question is similar to what happens with other sport phenomena (and legal practices)—these fouls demonstrate or are expression of the existing tension between a normative dimension and an applicable dimension. According to the first dimension, rules define some acts or plays as valid or not valid. But the second dimension asserts that the procedural rules are those that establish that the decisions of judges and referees (even with the acceptance of players and spectators) on the validity of plays are final and must be carried out. They express a convention (or ethos) about how to apply sport rules. On occasions, these decisions become generally accepted even though they are contrary to the content of the rules, which leads to an explanatory tension according to the point of view adopted on the sport phenomenon, sometimes nearer to the rules or sometimes closer to the conventions.

For this reason, the examination of strategic intentional fouls provides a touchstone for examining the moral significance of sport and especially its premier internal value: fair play. The analysis of fair play will be the object of the first section of this chapter. Later, I will take a close look at the structure of these fouls as well as how they differ from the similar phenomena of cheating and fraud. Finally, I will contemplate the legitimacy of strategic intentional fouls.

FAIR PLAY

One of the reasons that has driven sport to constitute one of the main activities of human beings lies in its moral function regarding individuals and society as a whole. In this way, it has been historically considered that sport allows individuals not only to better their physical and mental health, it also constitutes an arena for self-expression and self-development. But perhaps the most outstanding moral characteristic of sport is what has been called fair play.

Fair play is considered by most to represent the moral nucleus of sport. In spite of the difficulties that there may be in nailing down the precise meaning of this expression, it has a clear and powerful effect on rules and emotions. It displays its effects on the interpretation of the rules of the game as well as in the behavior that should be shown by athletes on the field of play (being a "good sport"). Fair play is the standard with an overarching reach over sports as a social practice and has a number of distinguishing traits: collaboration, equality, respect, recreational intent, etc. These traits are generally opposed to other ways of understanding sport, among which are competitiveness and the desire to win as primordial goals.

However, scholars have not been able to reach a consensus on the exact meaning of this expression. At different times fair play has been characterized as: a) a set of values; b) respect for the rules; c) respect for the agreement (or contract); or d) respect for the game. In the following sections, I will present on these meanings and end with a potentially more complete (and complex) reconstruction of the moral structure of fair play, which was put forward by the Norwegian philosopher of sport, Sigmund Loland.

Fair Play as a Set of Values

According to the first characterization of fair play, there may be a bag of virtues or attitudes that would apply to sport. According to some others, the list would contain virtues like compassion, equity (or justice), sportsmanship, and integrity (Butcher and Schneider 2001) which would come about as a result of moral reasoning applied to sport. Other characterizations include virtues like justice, honesty, responsibility, and charity on their lists of virtues.

The problem with this interpretation of fair play, according to Butcher and Schneider, is that it runs the risk of relativism since each author (or the culture of each sport) can offer a list of different virtues due to the fact that they start with a different conception of morals. By way of example, Kalevi Heiniläs has studied different interpretations of fair play in the sporting cultures of England, Sweden, and Finland. But perhaps the clearest point is explained in the anecdote told by Loland and MacNamee

(Loland and McNamee 2000) about a match between Arsenal and Sheffield. It was here that after one of Sheffield's players had recovered from
a blow, an African player who had recently been signed by Arsenal inter-
cepted the ball that an Arsenal player was returning to the Sheffield
defenders. Instead of returning the ball, he took it downfield and scored,
much to the astonishment of the Sheffield keeper. The surprise of the
African player in the face of this reaction was clearly due to the fact that
this player did not have the sense of fair play as the rest of the players in
this type of situation who act differently: they try to resume the state of
the game that was taking place prior to the injury. The question then
arises how these discrepancies which arise from different historical traditions and social contexts should be dealt with. Thus, Butcher and Schneider's focus:

> It is dismissed, as argued above, because it offers no defensible method
> of deciding which characteristics or actions should fall within the rele-
> vant definitions and no method of arbitrating between competing
> claims (Butcher and Schneider 2001; 24).

Fair Play as Respect for the Rules

A completely different focus than the one seen in the previous section
is the one that maintains that fair play should be characterized by respect
for the rules of the game, by the adaptation of the participants in a sporting competition to the "letter of the law," or the rules, in this case. This
justification is usually based on the idea that sports are institutional crea-
tions and activities guided by rules. Without rules, there would be no
games or sports.

However, the principle objection to this method of understanding fair
play is that is does not offer an appropriate characterization of sport. Our
shared intuitions on the phenomenon of sport do not make light of written rules. One way of expressing this could be through the famous example of a squash player. Let us imagine that a squash game will be played
and one of the participants, Josie, has forgotten her racket, which means
according to the rules that she will lose the game. However, her opponent
uses the same model, type, and size of racket, and she has two. But Josie
is a great competitor who could beat her and make her lose the championship. What should the rival do? The rules do not oblige her to lend
the racket . . . but fair play seems to suggest that she should. In this way,
this second conception of fair play cannot explain those actions that happen in the interests of fair play but that are not directly covered or regulated by the written rules.

Fair Play as an Agreement or Contract

One subsequent way of understanding fair play in sport is to explain it as based on a contract or agreement. Undoubtedly, the participants' agreement is one fundamental element in the aspect of competition: the participants tacitly (or expressly) agree from the outset to the way the respective skills will be measured as well as to what actions and tactics are allowed in the game. One way or another, the athletes consensually accept being bound by the rules of the same. In this way, they freely accept the authority of these rules and whatever arbiter or judge that the competition has to settle conflict between participants in a competition.

However, this characterization does not offer a complete overview of fair play, beyond what is entailed by the topics examined in previous sections. And this is the main objection to this approach: it is similar to the conception of fair play as respect for rules; that the idea of sport guided by contracts or agreements leads to reducing fair play to the literal notions laid out in contracts. This does not seem to have anything to do with the "spirit of the game." This is the vision of Butcher and Schneider.

Fair Play as Respect for the Game

Butcher and Schneider advocate an interpretation of fair play based on respect for the game. In spite of the fact that both terms are far from being easily defined, both authors highlight the fact that when respect is referred to, it should be understood in the sense of "honor," "value," and "esteem" of the game. That is, it represents a moral attitude regarding a particular object that goes beyond formal obedience toward the rules that comprise sports. Thus, given that games are created and governed by rules, they deserve to be honored, esteemed and valued (Butcher and Schneider 2001; 32).

It should be now clear that sport cannot be boiled down to written rules. It is also a set of social practices, in the sense of the MacIntyrean expression, which means that there are internal goods which are precisely the main object of respect and honor. For this author, a (social) practice is

> any coherent and complex form of socially established cooperative human activity through which goods internal to that form of activity are realized in the course of trying to achieve those standards of excellence which are appropriate to, and partially definitive of that form of activity, with the result that human powers to achieve excellence, and human conceptions of the ends and goods involved, are systematically extended (McNamee 1995; 233).

It does seem rather astonishing that, in order to give an example of a social practice, MacIntyre resorts to sport, specifically chess and soccer

(McNamee 1995). For the moment, let us leave the fact that this juxtaposition is not immune to criticism, but instead focus on the fact that he turns precisely to sport because it fulfils the characteristics that define a social practice in his understanding: a) the activity is interesting due to its intrinsic creativity; b) it is challenging, that is, it is not a simple activity, but rather one that is complex whose objects are not easy to accomplish; c) it is a freely chosen activity; and d) it is an activity that the participant has the ability to judge his own performance.

This assessment is clearly reminiscent of Aristotelian philosophy. For the authors in these practices, what is relevant is the existence of internal goods whose pursuit by the participants in sport contributes to improving and to driving meaning in the individual's own life.

But participation in a social practice assumes accepting these models of excellence in addition to obeying the rules. The pursuit of goods cannot be carried out separately from the established standards, but rather the criteria, preferences, and choices of the participants are subject to the authority of the rules. That is precisely what these authors wish to highlight with their characterization of fair play as respect for the game; that participants have to adapt their actions and attitudes to the features of the game itself as a practice. If a person decides to participate in a game, as soon as he or she does so, he or she is acquiring and taking on a new set of interests: "Those interests become interests of the athlete. If you respect the game, you honor and you take seriously the standards of excellence created and defined by that game. . . . Because such an athlete accepts the standards of soccer excellence, he or she would work to acquire and exhibit soccer skills" (Butcher and Schneider 2001; 34).

The main consequence of this attitude toward sport is when athletes start to practice a given sport, they pursue internal goods and are mostly motivated by them, and not by other factors or external goods, like fame and economic compensation.

From this characterization of fair play as respect for the game, several practical implications can be inferred. These implications refer to how games should be modelled in terms of allowed and dis-allowed actions on the field of play as well as the attitudes towards rivals and players' own commitments to the game. Following this line of thought, there ought to be a certain degree of equality between players, who should be trying to obtain the best from themselves; the final result of the competition should primarily be the product of the display of predicted abilities in the game itself; it should be played in accordance with the rules; the display of rivals' abilities should not be illegally impeded; opponents should not be seen as enemies but as facilitators of the display of excellence, etc.

If we now return to the case of Josie, the expected conclusion according to this view of fair play is that there are sufficient reasons for the opponent to lend the racket to the competitor, and in this way be able to compete in the squash match. In effect, if participants respect the game, they then have internal motivation to play. At the end of the game there is primarily an opportunity to enjoy the match and to test our skills. Additionally, Butcher and Schneider point out that the sport itself— squash in this case—"is enhanced by people competing and playing at their best whenever possible" (Butcher and Schneider 2001).

However, Butcher and Schneider's reconstruction warrants criticism for almost exactly the same reasons that they themselves use to create a vision of fair play as a set of values, given that social practices can be distinct in each community or culture. At the very least, a particular understanding of goods internal to sport can be generated in different contexts. In addition, a social practice can evolve and accept as correct actions those that are opposed to the original conventional framework, or from a critical-reflection point of view their validity may be doubtful.

A vision that attempts to avoid these criticisms is that of Sigmund Loland, who proposes a foundation for the moral value of fair play and of sport from an Aristotelian framework, but simultaneously avoids critiques regarding presumed relativism by incorporating universally defendable principles.

The Moral Structure of Fair Play: The Analysis of S. Loland

Even though the practical implications of Sigmund Loland's analysis of fair play are similar to those of Butcher and Schneider in that they both refer to Aristotelian philosophy as the foundation for understanding fair play. The approach of the Norwegian author is considerably more sophisticated, making it somewhat difficult to paraphrase; however, I will attempt to lay out the general features.

Loland's starting point is in some sense more broad since the question that he initially raises is what role sport plays in human life. Showing powerful influence from the Aristotelian tradition, he begins by hypothesizing that sport must be understood as a means or an environment for human flourishing and for that to happen, fair play must be structured as a moral system that allows the behavior of athletes in competitions to be guided:

> It suggests a re-articulation of a classic ideal for sport competitions, fair play, and argues that the realization of this ideal can make such competitions morally justifiable and indeed valuable activities in the broader perspective of human life. The claim is not that sport is a necessary part of human flourishing, but rather that, if practised according to fair play, sport can be one among the many activities that could contribute to such flourishing (Loland 2002; xiii).

From this point, Loland begins his argument that will lead him to give not only an exhaustive vision of sport and a complex overview of fair play, but he also details sports' concrete application in many fields of debate on athletic competitions, such as the classification in competitions based on sex and age, technical discussions on performance enhancement in sport, and the role of luck and merit in sport. Nevertheless, I will limit my treatment to the moral structure of fair play.

Following the detailed study of different moral conceptions, Loland attempts to arrive at an eclectic vision that allows one to realize the moral structure of sport. For support in this endeavor, he resorts to two strategies used in John Rawls' well-known constructivist procedure to arrive at the principles of justice that should govern a well-ordered society. The first well-known strategy is "reflective equilibrium"; the second, the characterization of human agents who decide the principles of justice (and those who these principles will apply to).

According to the first strategy, the "reflective equilibrium" allows moral principles to be attained that are balanced with the intuitions and the most abstract ideals that moral agents in a concrete context may aspire to. In this way, it is feasible "to search continuously for the best possible articulations in the particular contexts in which we find ourselves living and acting" (Loland 2002; 39). Said another way, the principles that Loland puts forward as contents of fair play do not coincide with basic intuitions that individuals in a society and culture have. Remember that this was one of the objections to fair play understood as a set of values, since these values can vary from one society to another. But neither should such principles be so far removed from basic intuitions. On the other hand, the principles that would inform fair play would be faulty for their abstractness or idealism, making them unworthy of being put into practice in any society or context.

According to the second strategy, moral agents should be characterized as informed and reasonable, respectful and free at the time of choosing the content of fair play.

Having put forward the philosophical basis of his proposal, Loland goes on to establish three basic principles of fair play, with the first one being a meta-norm to be used in case of conflict between the other two (Loland 2002; 39).

1. Choose norms that cannot be reasonably rejected as a basis for unforced, informed general agreement.
2. Maximize expected average preference satisfaction among all parties concerned.
3. Relevantly equal cases ought to be treated equally; cases that are relevantly unequal can be treated unequally, and unequal treatment ought to stand in reasonable accordance with the actual inequality between cases.

As I have pointed out above, these principles are the result of an eclectic conception of sport. While the second principle is clearly utilitarian, the third has a deontological slant, and together they represent complementary visions of ethical reasoning in sport.

According to Loland, these principles allow specific norms to be derived that can be used to realize from the main internal debates in sport, and at the same time, guide what is correct and right in sport. In this way, Loland tries to gloss over, on one hand, the conditions for justice using Rawls' Kantian focus by making using of a teleological Aristotelian focus centered on the development of "human flourishing." The last paragraph of his book sums up his response to the questions that was initially posed about the place of sport in human life:

> Hence, if practised in accordance to my norms for fair play, sport possesses special potential to provide an arena for human flourishing and so find a place as one among many possible practices constitutive of a good life (Loland 2002; 149).

Fair Play and Strategic Intentional Fouls

What makes strategic intentional fouls a topic of discussion is the adaptation of different understandings of sport. In this way, an understanding that adopts fair play as the moral core of sport, SIFs lack justification and they should be punished additionally so that players are not lured into committing them, given the fact that the moral framework of sport is opposed to committing fouls intentionally. They constitute an act against the goods internal to the sport among which are "be the best you can be" and the display of one's own abilities. This interpretation will be explained in detail below through the interpretativism presented by Fraleigh and Torres.

On the other hand, there are other characterizations of sport in which these fouls would form part of the game, of its ethos. They argue that in addition to fair play there are other elements that are equally important in the characterization of sport, like competition and the pursuit of victory. These factors combine to make SIFs a valid element of sport. But before examining this discussion, it is necessary in order to better clarify the types of fouls.

For the evaluative debate around SIFs, it would helpful to have a more precise definition of these fouls' structure as well as their limitations when compared to closely related issues, such as cheating and fraus legis. Finally, I attempt to show some difficulties in distinguishing SIFs from gamesmanship.

Committing a strategic intentional foul tends to be presented as a case of infraction upon the rules governing a sport (in the broad sense of the word). In effect, it is an intentional act for which the violator wants to be detected and punished, and as a result, expects some benefit in the competitive setting (Fraleigh 2007; 212). There are several concepts with which SIFs can be confused, namely fraus legis and cheating. In all three cases, the player intentionally tries to obtain a competitive advantage not permitted by the principles of sport practice.

Cheating

One of the issues is that SIFs are similar to is cheating. Although this concept is by no means simple to define, Loland's definition provides a useful starting point:

> [C]heating is an attempt to gain an advantage by violating the shared interpretation of the basic rules (the ethos) of the parties engaged without being caught and held responsible for it. The goal of the cheater is that the advantage gained is not eliminated nor compensated (Loland 2002; 96).

SIFs and cheating are similar in that in both cases the perpetrator is attempting to obtain an advantage in the game. A characteristic example of this occurs in soccer when a player fakes a foul in the opposing team's area to fool the referee. In this sense, most specialists agree that the opponents in both cases are not accorded proper respect, and they are put at a disadvantage. The basic principles governing sports are also disrespected and violated.

Nevertheless, one difference is relevant to both these concepts. In SIFs, the player carries out an infraction of the rules with the aim of being detected by the referee or judge. In addition, he is receptive to receiving the sanction that he will be given since it is in this way that he is able to obtain a competitive advantage in the game. This is not the case with cheating; here the athlete's core aim is to go unnoticed so that the cheating is not detected as such by the referee. This is the way the player can gain a competitive advantage.

SIF and Fraus Legis

Another concept that SIFs bear a certain similarity to is fraus legis, a Latin term meaning abuse or fraud of the law. This issue has been taken into account in many legal systems. Article 6.4 of the Spanish Civil Code establishes the following:

> The acts committed under the context of norms whose aim is to attain a prohibited objective for the legal system or contrary to it, should be considered to be carried out in fraus legis.

In this way acts, which legally constitute fraus legis, are prima facie allowed by norms, but when all factors are considered, legal decisions as a whole conclude that they are forbidden due to the principles that limit the justifiable scope of the rule in question.

In the sports arena, it could legally be considered fraus legis if it were the case that two soccer teams who both needed a point to not be sent to a minor league or to advance to the next round mutually decide not to hurt one another and to tie a match. In this way, they both meet their goals, even though they could be harming the interest of a third team and/or the principles of the sport that state that matches should be played with the intention of winning. Using this assumption, the formal and written rules do not impede (that is, they allow) playing defensively, but the teams are, in a sense, covered by the rules in that the rules would not find that the principles of the sport world had been defrauded. What is characteristic of fraus legis is that it connects the possibility of making use of legal norms to reach ends that were not contemplated by the law (Atienza and Ruiz Manero 2006; 68). In this way, the structure of fraus legis would consist of a behavior that apparently conforms to a norm (the so-called "pertinent norm"), but it would produce a result that is contrary to one or more norms or to the legal order as a whole (the "defrauded norm"). In the sport domain, the idea inherently central to sport is that it deals with competition linked to the pursuit of excellence in skills established by the rules. And this foundation serves to clarify actions that are acceptable and those that are not within the framework of sports. Actions that support and maintain contesting the rule-defined skills are acceptable while those that reduce or negate the contesting of those same skills are not (Fraleigh, 2007; 213).

Although there seems to exist a certain kinship between SIFs and fraus legis, due to the their two-component structure (the pertinent norm and the defrauded norm) and in both cases the action is carried out with the aim of obtaining a benefit that is not contemplated or prohibited by the normative system (in a broad sense), there is no real reason for them to be confused. The reason for this is that in fraus legis, the pertinent norm is a permitted norm is being used by the violator and it covers the action. Contrariwise, for SIFs, the relevant norm that is being used by the perpetrator to obtain a competitive advantage by making use of a norm that establishes a prohibition. Said another way, in fraus legis the perpetrator obtains an advantage not contemplated by the rule system through the use of a relevant norm established by the system itself; in SIFs, the violator obtains an advantage by breaking the rules.

Fraus legis could be better understood in countries belonging to the Common Law tradition as "spoiling the game" (Suits 1978; 47). This expression, however, is not easy to define. For example, Suits says: "spoilsports recognize neither rules nor goals" (Suits 1978; 47), and McFee characterizes spoiling the game differently, where the main point is that the sportsperson recognizes rules, but he/she gives a different use or interpretation of them, not according to the sport goals. McFee points out that the term spoiling "roughly characterize[s] behavior that, while not contrary to the rules of a game/sport, is nonetheless not how one ought to play it: for participating in the game or match should mean participating in ways that respect one's opponents, showing due regard for them."

Spoiling plays do not permit opponents the possibility of playing the game according to its spirit, a possibility one must grant to opponents who are taken seriously. Although permitted by the rules, such plays are recognized—at least by knowledgeable audiences—as inappropriate ways to play the game/sport: "an arena where players who 'spoil' may legitimately be criticized by the audience, team-mates and the media, but not by referees" (McFee 2004; 112–13). As I have said before referring to *fraus legis*, spoiling "comes about when there is a conflict between the letter of the rules (the written rules or statutes) and the spirit of the rules—that is, the principles (for instance, of fairness), on which the rules rest" (McFee 2004; 114). Although McFee is not precise enough here, I think we can understand that he is referring to spoiling of actions as ones permitted explicitly by norms or not regulated in the sport normative order, but that are contrary to moral principles of sport.

Structure of Strategic Intentional Fouls

As I mentioned rather tentatively above, SIFs are those acts that are intentional whereby the violator breaks a rule and fully expects to be detected and punished, and, in the end, as a result of this sanction hopes to obtain some benefit in the competitive situation. This is how Fraleigh characterizes the situation. Nonetheless, it is possible to examine this concept in greater detail and to highlight several significant aspects. Firstly, SIFs assume an axiological gap. Secondly, in SIFs the violator can be said to have special intentions or ulterior motives.

Strategic Intentional Fouls and Axiological Gaps

In reality, SIFs are cases where "axiological gaps" appear, that is, those situations in which it is deemed that the legislator or the general authority, which passes a law that regulates a case or situation, has not considered a circumstance or property that should have been taken into account because it is considered relevant.

It is necessary to distinguish between typical cases of gaps in rules and those that occur in axiological gaps. In the former, the case has been deemed relevant by the legislator but it is not explicitly regulated, i.e., there is no norm that establishes a normative solution for the case. In the case of "axiological gaps," however, there is a defect in the value placed on the case by the system: the case is regulated, but the solution should have been different because some important aspect did not receive the attention it deserved. Let us suppose that at the entrance to a hospital there is a sign that prohibits dogs from entering hospital grounds. At a given time, a blind person arrives at the hospital with his guide dog. Following the rule against the entrance of dogs, the guide dog must be denied access (the case is regulated; there is no gap in the rules), but many consider there to be an axiological gap since when those rules were established, there should have been certain exceptional situations taken into account, such as the case of dogs who serve as guides for visually impaired people.

In the case of SIFs, something similar occurs. The case is regulated: the legislator has considered that an action in the game should be regulated through a prohibition and discourages its performance by tying it to a sanction. Now there is an aspect in the carrying out of this behavior that the legislator has not predicted, and this is what generates the problem. The unforeseen aspect is that the violator expects to gain a competitive advantage with the foul. If the legislator had taken this circumstance into consideration, he probably would have regulated it. But this was not the case.

At the level of adjudication by the referees and umpires, the illegitimate gain obtained by the player through the SIF could be amended appealing to the internal principles of sport. As R. Dworkin suggests in the domain of the Law where judges could interpret the legal material as including not only rules but principles as well, the referee could appeal to principles in order to avoid the application of the (unjust) rule. Dworkin gives as example a case very similar to our SIFs:

> In 1889 in a New York court, in the famous case of *Riggs vs. Palmer*, had to decide whether an heir named in the will of his grandfather could inherit under that will, even though he had murdered his grandfather to do so. The Court began its reasoning with this admission: "It is quite true that statutes regulating the making, proof and effect of wills, and the devolution of property, if literally construed, and if their force and effect can in no way and under no circumstances be controlled or modified, give this property to the murderer." But the court continued to note that "all laws as well as all contracts may be controlled in their operation and effect by general, fundamental maxims of the common law. No one shall be permitted to profit by his own fraud, or to take advantage of his own wrong, or to found any claim upon his own iniquity, or to acquire property by his own crime." The murderer did not receive his inheritance (Dworkin 1978; 23).

In the domain of sport, a similar approach based in the idea of the integrity offered for principles to the normative system is due to Russell, who gives several Principles of Games Adjudication: 1) "Rules should be interpreted in such a manner that the excellences embodied in achieving the lusory goal of the game are not undermined but are maintained and fostered. . . . ; 3) Rules should be interpreted according to principles of fair play and sportsmanship; 4) Rules should be interpreted to preserve the good conduct of the games" (Russell 1999; 35–36).

Nonetheless, sometimes the sports authority tries to patch the gap. As Dixon points out, "The recent (but unevenly enforced) decision by FIFA (The Federation of International Football Associations) to automatically penalize an SIF by ejection from the game (without substitution) indicates that soccer's highest governing body regards it as a violation of the game's spirit" (Dixon 2003; 120–21). But, again in some cases the sanction could be seen as an insufficient attempt to honor the fairness of competition.

STRATEGIC INTENTIONAL FOULS AND SPECIAL INTENTION

The standard conception of an SIF indicates that it is an intentional act. So how can this intention be defined? If we turn to the answers offered in a Penal Code, we can see that a distinction is drawn between specific and general intent crimes. Most crimes are based on "general intent with a minimum of premeditation to carry out an action typified in the penal code." In a crime of general intent it needs only be demonstrated that a criminal act occurred; it is not necessary to prove the purpose or motive of the crime. An example would be a minimum intention to use force as in the case of common assault. X intends to injure Y, and to determine the realization of a criminal act under the penal code (actus reus), it suffices to prove that there was an assault on Y and that this was the intention of X, independently from other more removed objectives (e.g., revenge, hate, etc.).

A specific intent crime, on the other hand, requires the realization of a prohibited act (actus reus) but also the association with an intention or aim to go beyond the mere realization of the act. For example, in the crime of genocide, the perpetrator must actually commit the actus reus with the determined intention which goes beyond the mere realization of the actus reus. That is, the perpetrator has an ulterior motive. The former consists in carrying out an action whose result would be the actus reus (e.g., assassinating an individual) in which the subjective element is fulfilled with the wilful misconduct. The second intention more precisely would have the objective of doing away with the group to which the said subject belongs. The "intent to destroy" includes an additional subjective requirement that complements the general intention and goes beyond the basic objectives of the definition of a crime.

What is distinctive about SIFs is that the violator has, at the time of committing the foul that is taken into account in the normative system, a special or ulterior motive: not only committing the foul but also obtaining (illegitimately and not considered by the normative system) a competitive advantage. For an SIF, just as for genocide, it is the second intention that makes the individual's action decisive when committing the foul considered in the ordinances.

If we connect this aspect of SIFs, the special or ulterior intention of the perpetrator and the above-mentioned axiological gap, we can see the two main problems that surround SIFs (and the actions in fraus legis). In the first place, the addition of the special intention makes it in general more difficult to prove that the act is done with the desire to subvert the spirit of sport, since it is formed using mental elements to which an external agent does not have direct cognitive access (although shared indications can be established that allow its existence to be ascertained).

But the second problem is more important philosophically: how to distinguish them from gamesmanship, which is a slippery concept that we use to refer to the use of dubious although not technically illegal methods of obtaining a competitive advantage (trash-talking, taking an inordinate amount of time between points in a tennis match, etc.), if it is considered that it forms part of the game . . . in at least some of its expressions (Simon 2007; 225, Dixon 2003; 120).

Regarding this second question, there are some interesting examples. Some coaches decide to rest their traditional starting players to avoid fatigue, injury, or sanctions that could impede or reduce their participation in other matches where a title or a league is at stake. Their decision has effects that are similar to those of SIFs. Should they be qualified as gamesmanship or fraus legis? Should they be accepted or prohibited?

Another relatively frequent strategy currently in soccer, which I believe was first used by Johann Cruyff, is that of an offensive player provoking a corner kick when he or she has the ball close to the base line. Being flanked by defenders and considering that there is no chance to keep possession, the offensive player deliberately kicks the ball off the defender and out of bounds in order to provoke the corner kick. It is necessary to point out that here the constitutive skills are renounced in favor of a restorative ability, but circumstances allow a competitive advantage to be obtained against a rival. At the same time, this advantage is efficiently obtained in a difficult situation. Should this type of strategic decision be considered a kind of gamesmanship or a case of fraus legis? This action would seem to be a case of fraus legis as it takes advantage of the possibility to obtain a competitive advantage, but the way it is attained seems to violate the principles of the sport. Said another way, constitutive skills are used for the sake of restorative ones resulting in the action subverting the inner logic of the sport contest (Torres 2000; 86).

On the other hand, it could be argued that it is a clear case of acceptable gamesmanship. As a matter of fact, the action of Cruyff was celebrated as a creative and brilliant tactic and now is frequently used by footballers.

The distinction between fraus legis (and SIFs) and gamesmanship is blurred. The common trait of these practices is they distort the final goal of sport and for this reason, making use of some of Suits' words, we can say that they show "an excess of zeal in seeking to achieve the . . . goals" (Suits 1978; 46). That excess of zeal is not as strong as that of the cheater who infringes on the rules. This is the difference between both phenomena. The practice of gamesmanship, SIF and fraus legis recognize sport rules, but in a different way than a "normal player" does: rules are considered not as a goal in and of themselves, but as a means to achieve an advantage in the game. Rules do not deserve honor in and of themselves; they are prices that must be paid to reach the goals. Here it becomes necessary to take conflicting sport principles under consideration, and umpires are given an irreducible domain in which their discretion is to be exercised (Russell 1999; 27). But this problem deserves a more detailed discussion that is not possible within the confines of this chapter.

To summarize I have analyzed SIFs with a view to providing a deeper understanding of the structure of such fouls, stressing the differences with closely related concepts: cheating, and especially fraus legis or what in Anglo-Saxon culture is called "spoiling the game." It seems clear that these two last phenomena share a common characteristic: the player that commits a foul with the intention of obtaining an advantage in the game that is disallowed by the sport legislation (in a broad sense). In both cases, the action subverts the spirit of the game because it intends to obtain a competitive advantage contrary to the internal principles of the game. However, it seems interesting and useful to point out that while with the fraus legis (or spoiling) the player intends to obtain the competitive advantage through an action in accordance with a permissive norm, with the SIF the player carries out an action forbidden by sport rules, but does it instrumentally: he wants to be sanctioned and obtain a competitive advantage (whether it be immediate or delayed in time).

In the second part I have tried to identify two features of the internal structure of SIFs: they assume an axiological gap and a "special intent." Both characteristics are those that turn these fouls into "hard cases." In the first place, the special intent makes it more difficult to test that the action is carried out with the intention of obtaining an ulterior goal beyond infringing on the concrete rule. Second, the existence of the axiological gap adds a difficulty as it entails that the player subverts the spirit of sport with such fouls. Analogously to what Dworkin proposes in the Law, some authors suggest principles (explicit or latent) that prevent players from obtaining competitive advantages derived from illegal actions. This second problem is evaluative: it presupposes that SIFs subvert internal principles of sport. However, this notion is challenged by a number of authors: in some cases, SIFs (even fraus legis actions) are accepted by the participants themselves as part of the game. In that sense, SIF and fraus legis actions are closer to gamesmanship: actions that are dubious but not necessarily illegal in the game. For this reason, these sorts of hard cases probably need to be examined on an individual basis in order to conclude if they are strongly contrary to the sport principles or are simply examples of strategies allowed by the sport practice.

RESPONSES TO STRATEGIC INTENTIONAL FOULS

Having examined the structure of SIFs, it is now feasible to examine how their structure has been analyzed and how they should be evaluated. There are three answers that involve completely different ways of understanding the field of sports: a) the formalist response; b) the response based on the "ethos of sport" (conventionalism); and c) the responses of interpretativism (or "broad internalism"). However, the first response, formalism, is not a proper response since its conceptual framework cannot actually account for SIFs.

The Formalist Response

The formalist explanation establishes that the rules for sport are its definition. The rules written and created through an established procedure are those that mold the purpose and meaning of sports. That is, what counts as a valid move or corrective action within the framework of the sport in question, whether it is scoring or committing a foul, is determined and specified by the sport in question.

Abiding by this characterization, the formalist position has a tough time accounting for SIFs within its conceptual framework. That a player commits an SIF implies that he or she is not playing the game, and that logically, the chance to win is eliminated. A different game is played when formalist rules are prescribed: potentially the chance to compete is annulled; or rather, a defective form of the game established by the rules ends up being played. In this way, for the formalist point of view on sport, with SIFs the game stops being played (Fraleigh 2007; 209).

The problem with formalism is that its characterization of fouls, whether they be SIFs or not, offers a version of the game that is not intuitive since every time a player violates a rule, he or she would be playing either a different game or a defective version of the original game. The objections raised against this formalist focus on sport point out that it forgets or does not consider that, in addition to the formal rules laid out within the basic regulatory framework, sports involve a set of social conventions and principles that govern the interpretation of codified rules in particular cases.

The reaction against formalism has led to two opposing conceptions, conventionalism and interpretativism.

Conventionalism and the Ethos of Sport

The approach to the phenomenon of sport based on the ethos of sport assumes the possibility of distinguishing two differentiated levels, with one based on rules and the other on conventions. As Fraleigh points out, different interpretations of ethos of sport exist according to the author who is cited. In this way for D'Agostino (D'Agostino 1995), ethos are conventions that determine how formal rules are applied in concrete circumstances; for Leaman and Lehman, they are ways in which players and spectators perceive the rules; for Tamburrini, they are the particular understanding of the game by the players.

Leaman is wary of both the formalist conception of sport in which following the rules becomes a core element and of the vision of fair play as a platonic entity in regulating play. In his opinion, the vision of sport should be realistic and attend to the different disciplines that are kept up-to-date by the leading actors, the athletes.

For Tamburrini, there should be an understanding of sport in which ethos are enlarged to account for how it is really played. This is the situation when in the concrete case of cheating; the unorthodox and radical conclusion is that in certain circumstances cheating should be validated. Despite the fact that this might be anti-sportsperson-like action or it might violate the rules, these practices are at the disposal of those who practice a sport" (Tamburrini 2000; 44). In keeping with this conception, the Argentine author arrives at the conclusion that some cheating forms part of the ethos of the game, at least in certain concrete practices. In effect, some cheating is relatively widespread among athletes in some disciplines (e.g., using hands to touch the soccer ball is an action that many players attempt). But its validation would be subject to certain conditions; that no harm is produced to other players and that an increase in the hedonistic potential of the game is produced. In other words, it implies the expression of a skill that makes the game somewhat more exciting. Consequently, in the final point of his argument, he validates the legitimacy of Maradona's historic goal against England in the 1986 World Cup, which provides the background for the title of his book that gives a different outlook on the sport: *The "Hand of God"?: Essays in the Philosophy of Sport*.

Beyond the differences that may exist in the characterization of ethos in sport, there are several objections. First of all, it is far from being clear that there is a widely accepted and practiced convention among participants in sport regarding SIFs. Of course, the effects of SIFs could be examined in great detail by inspecting the degree of acceptance and application of each type. In this way, some would be more widespread than others. For example, fouls a few minutes before the end of a basketball game seem to be more accepted than fouls at other times in the game. On the contrary, provoking yellow cards to complete the sanction in an unimportant match does not seem to be so popular. Some coaches seem to agree to using this tactic but others are opposed, due to the fact that it goes against the notion of fair play. In sum, there is a certain amount of disagreement that makes it difficult to make the case that such actions are valid because they are conventionally accepted by players.

In the second place, the acceptance of this approach to sport does not mean automatically accepting the correction of SIFs. Said another way, the practice can be empirically valid, but the logical leap cannot be made that accepting their existence would allow deriving their moral validity. A recurring critique is that the adoption by the majority of a particular ethos by a community in a certain social practice does not imply that it is fair, correct, appropriate, or that it should, in a larger sense, prevail. Similar to what happens in other social contexts, "social morality no matter how widespread it is, can be wicked, arbitrary, irrational, etc." In the arena of sport, this can be translated as shared sport "ethos" may encourage violence, discrimination among athletes, etc. Should an ethos, no matter how common it is among the participants, bolster these results? It seems that it should not.

In the third place, conventionalism has not stopped being a descriptive conception of sport, which lacks the ability to establish critical-reflexive elements that would allow moral validity to be established in its interpretativism practices. It can only limit itself to claiming that it is a practice regulated by norms and that it is understood in a certain way by participants, but it cannot critique dominant conventions. From this claim, critics of conventionalism can derive two additional problems: relativism and conservatism. Relativism arises because each community of athletes can contingently adopt an interpretation different from practice. On the other hand, in conventionalism itself there are no external elements that allow critiquing an adopted practice. For example, in soccer regulations pushing and grabbing among players in the penalty area are prohibited acts. And fans well know that before a corner kick, it is quite rare that these actions do not occur. And, referees rarely call this behavior, but rather at most they limit themselves to warning the players in the middle of the scuffle. The matter at hand is that players' carrying out of these actions and the tolerance of most referees tarnishes the game and provokes violence on many occasions between players. However, from the posited conventionalist positions, it is difficult to critique them given that the meaning of the rules comes from the convention itself.

Strategic Intentional Fouls and Interpretativism

Interpretativism has come to defend a conception of sport that goes beyond written rules and conventions by alleging the need to appeal to principles and values that critically endow the practice of sport with meaning. In this way for example, Butcher and Schneider claim that the meaning of the game derives from the "respect for the game"; for Loland it is linked to fairness, and Morgan refers to MacIntyre and his idea of good internal social practices.

These points of view demonstrate a central point inherent to sport: competition linked with the pursuit of excellence in skills established by rules. And this is the foundation to clarify what actions are acceptable and which are not within the framework of sport. Actions that support and maintain competition in the skills governed by these values are acceptable, while those that reduce or deny them are not. For this reason, authors like Fraleigh do not accept SIF as valid (Fraleigh 2007; 213).

However, as will be seen below, there is no logical or empirical need to maintain that these are the only values that are internal to sport. There are other authors who differ on these points of view and highlight that the values of sport itself have to do with the show and the victory, and based on them, SIFs may be considered differently. Let us examine these two points of view. I will take reflections by Fraleigh and César Torres into account within the scope of interpretativism that is favorable to SIFs. Then I will turn to different points of view, especially based on Simon's claims.

SIFs from the Perspective of Sport as a Display of Excellence

According to Fraleigh, when sport is at its best, competitions should be decided based on the exercise of constitutive abilities, which are abilities that make up the central logic of the sport. Following the distinction made by César Torres, in sport it is feasible to distinguish between two types of rules, depending on what the goal is: constitutive skills and restorative skills. Constitutive skills "define and shape the character of games" (Torres 2000; 86). Additionally, these abilities are seen as necessary to be able to overcome hurdles that the game itself establishes. The achievement of these skills constitutes the ideal of excellence in each sport. In this way, for example, in basketball these abilities include dribbling, scoring points, etc.; in soccer, striking the ball, dribbling, etc. Normally these are the skills that make the sport attractive, and this is what allows it to be explained that players enjoy the game and spectators are interested in its development.

On the other hand, restorative rules have a different objective:

> They prescribe precise penalties and methods for re-establishing the lusory project, but in doing so they generate additional skills that are employed during what may be labelled the regulative phase of a game, the period during which an interruption occurs and a need arises to put the game back on track (Torres 2000; 85).

Although these skills are important, they are secondary to the game. It could exist without them.

Thus, for authors like Fraleigh and Torres, provoking an SIF cannot be considered a constitutive skill in any sport. If sport is understood as a social practice established by a system of rules with internal goods and defining standards of excellences, then SIFs are revealed as inappropriate. This is not only because the means used to obtain them are expressly prohibited in the rules, but also because they subvert the teleological structure of the sport. While sports are configured to establish evaluations regarding the competitors' constitutive abilities and skills, committing an SIF entails ruining the game since it undermines and perverts the main challenge that is established in the practice of sport. For example, spectators would have reason to complain if a player on a team commits an intentional foul on a rival player in order to deliberately block a goal. Such a player would not be testing his or her constitutive resources and abilities, but would rather be impeding the opposing player from displaying his or her own abilities.

Strategic Intentional Fouls from the Perspective of the Sport and the Pursuit of Victory

It seems evident, as Fraleigh and Torres as well as Loland and other authors have tried to show, that sport is linked to measuring, comparing and evaluating competitors in the development of sporting events, that is, to what degree they attain excellence. This is what would be considered as part of its internal goods. There is little to be discussed in this regard.

However, sport also includes other aspects that appear to be core to its internal structure, among them: 1) competitiveness and pursuit of victory, along with all that this implies in the planning of strategies to reach it; 2) the excitement in the development of the competition (and with that, the greater enjoyment by spectators).

I think I have faithfully interpreted R. Simon in his defense of what he calls judicious strategic fouls. In his framework, he highlights that there can be strategic fouls that are contrary to the internal goods of the sport and that these ruin the competition by subverting constitutive skills. But not all SIFs are like this; there may be some that can be considered judicious; that is, instead of debasing the technical abilities of players, they could increase them, and simultaneously improve the excitement potential of the game.

Simon uses three core arguments. Firstly is his argument to reject SIFs which would also be applied not only to fouls, but also to strategies (which use strategic skills) that some teams could use to disrupt the display of rivals' superior constitutive skills and that destroy the corrective technical action that competition provides. For example, in soccer perhaps some teams could be disqualified for using "catenaccio" (a tactical system with a strong emphasis on defense) on rivals with more technical skills. In this way, in many teams using this tactic they aim for a tie in order to settle the score based on penalty kicks. But this style of game also uses constitutive skills (tactical order, skills, physical strength, psychological strength, etc.). Thus, the final score of the match is decided on penalty kicks, i.e., by using a restorative skill. To imply, as the argument of

Torres-Fraleigh seems to do, that "catenaccio" may be contrary to the spirit of the game would seem to be counterintuitive.

The second argument attempts to distinguish uses that can be accorded to SIFs, some of which are clearly illegitimate while others are not. Among the former, for example, grabbing a player who is about to score a goal due to his or her greater technical skill. Alternatively, there can be situations where the use of SIFs may be judicious. The example used by Simon is the following (Simon 2007; 225); in basketball games where the teams are equally balanced in terms of their constitutive abilities, it would not be inappropriate for the less skilled team to commit an intentional foul in order to make the rival miss their free throws. In this way, they would gain the opportunity to get an advantage in the game by gaining possession of the ball.

Thirdly, in some cases restorative skills require technical abilities similar to those required by constitutive skills, thus the talents and technical command needed for their use should not always be disdained.

Simon concludes that not all SIFs are necessarily inappropriate from an ethical point of view. It should be seen whether certain conditions are present (Simon 2007; 225):

1. That rivals are on equal terms regarding their constitutive skills. If this is the case, it would seem appropriate to resort to restorative skills (e.g., free throws) to settle the equality.
2. That the team that commits a strategic foul has no other choice based on the use of constitutive skills that would give it a reasonable chance to win.
3. That the penalty for the foul should reasonably be considered the price for the act, more than a punishment; that is, the penalty that will have to be reasonable compensation for the offended team.
4. That the perpetrator of the strategic foul ought not obtain an advantage in the game if the adversaries would have won through the exercise of their constitutive skills.

The conclusion that Simon finally arrives at is that strategic fouls are not contrary to the internal values of sport and that they additionally increase the excitement of the game:

> The judicious use of strategic fouls in basketball games raises the competitive intensity of the game, making it a better test for the players, and if restorative skills can help determine which of two otherwise evenly matched opponents is superior, such fouls can have a defensible place in the game (Simon 2007; 226).

I agree with Simon on general terms:

1. It is preferable to examine the legitimacy of SIFs on a case-by-case basis and not catalogue them as legitimate or illegitimate as a whole.

2. I think some cases they constitute a legitimate use of a competitive strategy by a player or a coach.
3. The criteria for acceptability that he proposes for assessing SIFs seem to be appropriate and reasonable.

CONCLUSIONS

In this chapter I have tried to offer distinct approaches to the moral nature of sport. In the first section, I have focused on presenting what is at the core of sports' moral structure: fair play. Given the controversial nature, I have laid out the principle conception of fair play.

In the second section, I have analyzed strategic intentional fouls. This element of sport is not only interesting in and of itself, it has also served as a touchstone to compare the vision of sport derived from fair play with other conceptions that underline the importance of other elements in sport: competiveness and the desire to win. In this way, I have attempted to deal with the structure of fouls in depth, highlighting their differences with the similar concepts of gamesmanship and cheating, as well as stressing one assumption about special intent and an axiological gap.

In the second part of this chapter, I have placed my attention on its justification. To do this, I have analyzed several responses including formalism, conventionalism and interpretativism. After discarding formalism and conventionalism, I have examined the interpretativism-based responses that highlight the illegitimacy of this type of fouls. In my view, what I have tried to argue can be summed up in that sport, in addition to being a pursuit of excellence, has other internal goods and core components, among them competiveness and the pursuit of victory, with all that is implied by the use of these strategies. Additionally, SIFs should be analyzed on an individual basis so as not to carry out a generalized negative evaluation of them. Some expressions of SIFs exist that do not entail a grave threat to the value of sport in terms of expression of constitutive skills and the pursuit of excellence. They involve, rather, a strategic decision by the athlete who, when contemplating the balance of advantages and disadvantages, can consider what is acceptable according to the rules and principles of the game.

TWO

Doping

Few topics in the field of sports have had as much social impact or have been debated as much as doping. This discussion has not only taken place in academic circles, it has also been avidly discussed on the streets themselves. Even though this is not strictly a new phenomenon, in the last twenty years it has received an unusual amount of attention due primarily to the fact that popular sport icons have been tainted by the suspicion (or certainty) of having taken substances that illegally improved their sport performance. The list of doping victims is extraordinarily long, despite the fact that it has certainly not affected all types of sport to the same extent. Some sports, cycling and track and field in particular, have taken quite a beating from this phenomenon.

Another aspect worthy of mentioning is the mismatch of opinions between the parties involved. Historically doping has been condemned by the majority of athletes, sport authorities and society in general because it is viewed as a way to gain an illegitimate advantage over rivals and because it poses a health risk to the individual athlete. Nonetheless, in the last decade a growing number of voices have been heard that critically question the anti-doping policy of domestic and international bodies. Those same voices have also pointed out that from a moral standpoint, the reasons for stigmatizing doping merit a meticulous review: there may not be reasons to so severely condemn athletes' consumption of substances or undergoing enhancement treatments under certain conditions. So, the questions to be explored are: Why are enhancement treatments prohibited for athletes but are permitted for all other individuals? Are there relevant differences between therapeutic and enhancement treatment? Should all enhancement treatments and all sporting disciplines be considered the same? Do all the arguments based on protecting athlete health and those based on protecting the sport deserve to be given equal weight?

But before we delve into these issues, let us explore the origin of this term. There is a certain amount of doubt regarding the origin of the term doping. According to Verroken, it is likely that it comes from the term "dop" was used in South Africa in the 1700s to refer to a stimulant alcoholic beverage. Others point out that it may come from the Dutch term "doop" which later came to the English language to designate a substance with sedative and hallucinogenic effects. At the end of the nineteenth century, the term was used to refer to beverages with narcotic effects, and at the turn of the twentieth century, it began to be used in reference to enhancement of physical performance, although initially it referred to the enhancement of race horses.

In modern times, the search to improve performance in sports, in order to reach new goals in accordance with the Olympic motto, seems to be an inherent element to the practice of sport and the attitude of the athlete. "Citius, altius, fortius" is the Latin phrase meaning "faster, higher, stronger," the motto of the Olympic Games. For many years, this motto was based on the assumption that improvement in athletic competition could only be obtained through training, sacrifice, and perfection of natural gifts as could be carried out by the individual athlete. It seemed that sport ethics were linked to these values, which also served to develop the athlete's own sense of morality. But it is true that the spirit of the sport has always driven athletes to try new methods of improving themselves beyond pure training and personal effort.

It is not surprising that evidence has been found that some Greek athletes from classic times were using stimulants to improve their performance (Verroken 2005; 22) and that in the modern Olympics in 1904, it was known that the marathon winner, Thomas Hicks, took Strychnine injections during the race (Verroken 2005; 21). Some years before, the first (known) death due to doping took place in a cycle race between Bordeaux and Paris (1896). Since then, the practice of doping has been common in sport.

Several sources of data indicate how extensive this practice had become. In 1968 a member of the U.S. track and field team estimated that one-third of the team had used steroids in the training fields before the Games, and in 1988, at the Seoul Olympic Games, one coach predicted 40 percent of the women's track and field team had used steroids. The use and abuse of doping by the Olympic teams of several Eastern European countries has also been well documented. The unrestrained use of anabolic steroids consequently led to several female athletes not only developing characteristically male features, but actually augmenting them. Some eventually chose to undergo sex change operations, as was the case of the East German athlete Heidi Krieger, now Andreas Krieger. In other cases, unfortunately, some athletes who were the target of those practices died as a result of them.

Sport authorities were the first to take action against the enhancements arising from athletes' use of chemical substances to obtain better scores and times. This was likely the first area in which the physical enhancements through the use of doping were legally regulated. Already in 1928 the International Amateur Athletics Federation prohibited doping, and the International Olympic Committee (IOC) began to carry out mandatory doping testing in 1968. Since then many have called attention to the fact that this "war on doping" has a marked prohibitionist spirit. As a result of this attitude of absolute prohibition on doping, the World Anti-Doping Association (WADA) was created in 1999; one of its first decisions dealt with a new form of doping that had arisen in the past decade: gene doping.

In the Athens Olympic Games of 2004, systematic anti-doping tests were established for the first time. At that time, 3,000 drug tests were performed, 2,600 urine tests and 400 blood tests. Prohibited substances were found in the results of twenty-three athletes. Among all of the disciplines, weight lifting stood out for having eleven competitors excluded for the consumption of doping substances (Gracia Marco et al. 2009; 4).

Arguments for the Prohibition of Doping

The current anti-doping policy is quite widespread due principally to the influence of the dominant international and domestic sport authorities. The International Olympic Committee mentions three core values on which the (different versions of the) doping ban is based: the protection of athlete health (prevention of harm), clean competition (equity and avoidance of cheating), and the integrity and unity of sport (the values intrinsic to the practice of sport).

Nevertheless, the points of view generally held by the IOC and WADA have been widely discussed by some experts in the field who question the foundations of those three arguments and who point out other problems with the current ban policy. They point especially to the lack of clear criteria on the banned substances list and the counterproductive effects that this persecutionary policy itself has (an analogy has been drawn between the "Dry Laws" and a rise in clandestine usage). In light of this, I will lay out my arguments regarding the doping ban and the associated problems. Then I will go on to analyze the objections that have been mentioned.

The Problem with Cheating and the Effect on Equality

This argument is used to highlight that doping would be an infraction of the rules of the sport and that, therefore, whoever used substances or techniques to improve their athletic physical capacity would be committing a violation of those rules.

Regarding this argument that the use of enhancement drugs is supposed to have on athletic performance, other authors have pointed out that their use would also severely affect the principle of equality or fairness that should reign over the practice of any sport. Athletes who have taken part in doping would acquire advantages in their physical performance that their rivals would not have, thus damaging the principle of equality that governs sporting competitions.

In the first place, the cheating argument establishes that doping should be prohibited because it is contrary to the rules of the sport, and for this reason there is cheating. But it seems clear that this is a petitio principii fallacy (Schneider and Rupert 2009; 193): "If cheating means rule-breaking, then using banned substance or practice is cheating. It follows that gene doping, as a form of cheating, is wrong."

To break this vicious circular cycle, the rules would only need to be changed to allow this kind of activity. At the heart of this issue is whether moral reasons (or health, or public order, or reasons of any other kind) exist that justify the doping ban. If it is concluded that they do exist, then reasons for combating doping would be ones of morality, health, public order, etc., and not the strictly formalist question of a violation of a legal rule. Said another way, instead of considering doping as a mala prohibita (wrong because it is prohibited) practice, it is necessary to prove mala in se (wrong in and of itself).

With regard to the supposed effect on equality that doping has, there are three counter-arguments to be considered given the fact that current sport practices nevertheless allow other types of inequalities to exist.

The Genetic Lottery Argument

Sports measure certain types of inequalities, whether they be natural physical talents, abilities of strength or endurance, psychological determination, etc. Said another way, inequality per se is not unacceptable or unfair in sport. What's more, it could even be said that these inequalities form a vital part of sport. In fact, sport would be rather boring if it did not measure and even reward differences existing between athletes.

It has also been pointed out repeatedly that there is no such thing as a level playing field for all aspects of the game, given that some have benefited more than others from the genetic lottery of physical talents: some individuals are born with greater musculature, others with better endurance tendencies, and still others are endowed with speed. The clearest example is that of the Finnish skier Eero Maentyranta. In 1964 he won three gold medals. Afterwards, it came to light that he had a genetic mutation that allowed him to "naturally" have 40 to 50 percent more red blood cells than the average person. Was it fair that he had a significant advantage that he had obtained by chance? And what about the case of the British runner Charles Wegelius who was excluded and then later cleared of all charges in 2003? His spleen had been removed after an accident, and since this organ eliminates red blood cells, its absence results in elevated RBC levels (percentage of red blood cells in the blood), which leads to better physical performance. Athletes with a naturally higher red blood count level cannot participate in a race unless doctors carry out a battery of tests to prove that the level is in fact naturally occurring.

It is clear that sport does not only measure these abilities; it assumes them. A sport where all of the participants are of equal ability would not only be boring, it would possibly be absurd.

On the other hand, Savulescu has flipped this objection highlighting that doping could in fact provide relative equality to athletes and in this way overcome the arbitrary inequality resulting from the natural lottery. Appealing to the unfair results that would be brought about by doping in favor of the athlete who has been treated rather than the one who has not is a relatively weak argument. If we attend to the current historical context, sporting competitions would also be considered unfair, given the different genetic lottery that the different athletes have. In the current state of affairs, athletes make enormous efforts at training and improving their physical prowess but are incapable of defeating the rival who is lucky enough to be better genetically endowed. The matter at hand is, would it not be more just and more equitable to the practice of sport if there were greater equality generated by doping techniques and if victory did not depend solely on this factor, but rather on effort, excellence of character, and on technical skills?

The Wealth Argument

Another factor that favors the unjustifiable inequality in current athletic competitions is also random, but it is not questioned by sport authorities: being born in a rich country or a poor one. Obviously, the chances that athletes with better physical performance are quite distinct depending on the country they are in. Take this example: Australia was able to raise itself up to fourth place on the total medal count in the Athens Olympics thanks to massive government investment. The authors of one study estimate the cost of each medal at $32 million (Savulescu, Foddy and Clayton 2004; 13).

The Argument for the Relative Irrelevance of Doping

Lastly, the criticism that states the physical improvements would be so exaggerated that there would be no equality among athletes is nothing other than a caricature of the potential impact of genetic technologies in the practice of sport. Doping, at least in its current state (and in the near and foreseeable future) does not offer miraculous results to athletes through the simple ingestion of a pill or modification of a gene in order to provide the athlete extraordinary results. On the contrary, athletes would need to continue training and making sacrifices to finally obtain good results. Doping only offers a small step towards attaining better scores and, therefore, an athlete who trusts in miraculous results from a pill and stops practicing could hardly become part of the elite.

On the contrary, the success of many athletic disciplines does not depend only on a physiological factor, but rather on a variety of physical factors (speed, strength, power, endurance, etc.), mental factors (the ability to put together strategies and tactics) and psychological factors. The fact that a drug or a doping treatment can better one aspect of physical performance cannot guarantee at all that an athlete will be victorious or simply better than his or her rivals. While cases of doping are well-known in the cycling arena, it should be remembered that there are also many cyclists who took banned substances yet never won races or even stages.

In this way, the doping policy should listen and pay great attention to the distinct effects that substances and enhancement techniques have on each discipline and then establish particular criteria for each of them in terms of the circumstances that have been analyzed.

The Argument of Harm and Unjustified Paternalism

Authors who generally are against doping have pointed out that these practices may involve some type of harm, whether to the individual athlete or to other athletes in general.

The Harm to One's Self

One of the most frequently uttered arguments against doping is that athletes need protection from damage to their health or even risk to their lives. Following this line of thought, it is traditionally argued that substances or doping practices can negatively affect one's health, whether from taking uncontrolled amounts due to lack of medical supervision or because not enough is currently known about the long-term effects on the body (Anderson 2009; 5). Other versions of this argument highlight the fact that athletes are not in the best position to make independent and rational decisions because, in certain cases, they are not sufficiently informed as to the effects of these substances and doping techniques. In other cases, they may have taken substances because of external pressure or even coercion from coaches, managers, sporting authorities or even the pressure of the environment itself. One statistic suffices to show the effects of consuming doping substances: in 1987, when the consumption of

Erythropoietin (EPO) was at its height, it is estimated to have caused the death of twenty cyclists.

Faced with the objection that doping affects health detrimentally, it must be pointed out that the argument of unjustified paternalism is nevertheless relevant due to its infringement upon on the free will and decision-making ability of a rational adult human being (Moller 2010; 118).

The classic anti-paternalistic argument establishes that the only legitimate reason for the State to coercively interfere with individuals' autonomous decision-making abilities is to avoid harm to third parties. In this way, the appeal based on the welfare of the individual through the use of coercion does not constitute a good reason for limiting an individual's decision-making ability. Applying this argument to athletes, it is clear that their freedom to take (currently banned) doping substances, even when these may pose certain risks to their health, is infringed upon. All bans on these substances based on the argument that they can negatively affect an athlete's health would constitute a case of unjustified paternalism.

Additionally, if these paternalistic concerns are justified with regard to doping, sporting authorities ought to show the same zeal with regard to the risks that other practices entail: exceedingly intense training that provokes physical injuries and even death in certain sports (mountain climbing, boxing, weight lifting, skiing, etc.) clearly has a larger number of victims than doping. In other words, the doping ban is not only inconsistent, it could also be considered hypocritical (Schneider and Rupert 2009; 195).

In spite of this, some authors who favor lifting the doping ban also highlight the subtleties to this section focusing specifically on protecting athlete health. Savulescu highlights that it is important to know if the health risks are excessive or not. While he is tolerant of doping techniques that entail a slight or moderate risk to the physical integrity of the athlete, he advocates for maintaining current limits when the risk is excessive. Based on these suppositions, the athletes' health is put ahead of their freedom. Savulescu uses the example of blood EPO levels to support his position.

Another version that this paternalistic argument uses to favor the current doping ban is that athletes do not have the ability to be adequately informed of the (especially negative) consequences that may arise from the consumption of doping substances. In other words, they lack necessary information and therefore their decision to take doping substances or treatments cannot be completely autonomous.

Tamburrini challenges this line of thought. He accepts that we do effectively know very little about the effects of doping. We do know that in the long term, uncontrolled use of some performance-enhancing substances is detrimental to health, but at present we lack knowledge on the effects of sporadic doping without medical supervision. For this reason, at first blush, the objection is reasonable: athletes who take doping substances would be making decisions about vital topics without being fully informed (Tamburrini 2000b; 18).

There are also several arguments that oppose this objection. Firstly, not all performance enhancing methods fall into this category. For example, in terms of caffeine and blood doping, it is possible to claim that we likely have the fundamental knowledge necessary about their effects and this entails that it is reasonable for one to make informed decisions about them.

Secondly, with regard to ignorance as to the effect of doping due to athletes' negligence in researching relevant facts, this could be easily resolved with periodic encounters informing athletes about these aspects. These encounters could be required, with the consequence of not attending being the athlete's ban from taking part in athletic competitions.

Lastly, regarding performance enhancing methods that could be harmful even under medical supervision (e.g., anabolic steroids, growth hormone, etc.), our current lack of knowledge about direct results could be a direct result of the ban itself. Thus, more than supporting the ban, the present objection could be utilized to permit doping together with the necessary medical supervision. In other words, if the lack of knowledge is the problem, the abolition of the prohibition is undoubtedly a good strategy to ascertain the actual risks of doping (Tamburrini 2000b; 17).

The third version of this paternalistic argument consists in pointing out that athletes could be influenced or even coerced by trainers, managers, representatives, physicians, or sports authorities to take part in doping practices (Moller 2010; 127). It is well known that within elite sports there are tremendous economic and political powers at play that may not only affect the individual athletes but may also have repercussions on the whole entourage of people who surround them. It is not only the athlete who benefits from good results; rather, the effects of these results expand to include the people in the athlete's environment. And given that athletes already have the idiosyncratic tendency of trying to obtain the best results whatever the cost, the likelihood that they succumb to doping practices (with or without consent) is high.

This is the argument of Sigmund Loland:

> In real life, the theory seems naive. A core premise is the view of the empowered individual making free and informed choices. However, as are demonstrated by sociological analyses of the social context of doping, elite athletes are embedded in complex networks of power relations. No athlete is an island with full freedom to choose. In early stages of their career in particular, young athletes depend more or less totally upon good advice and guidance from coaches and support systems. Moreover, the survival of support systems depends upon sport success (Loland 2009; 157).

Tamburrini draws the analogy between the paternalistic measures imposed on other jobs or professions, for example, construction workers' compulsory wearing of a helmet. He argues that if this regulation did not exist, employers could coerce workers to not wear helmets. In fact, they could even turn this into a condition for employment in order to reduce costs. Workplace safety regulations purport to avoid cases of unfair coercion. In this way, the ultimate motivation is not to protect workers from their own decisions, but rather to protect them from being compelled by employers to take on risks that they do not wish to take.

Therefore, given the current state of professional sport where athletes are oftentimes supremely motivated to get the best results, the economic incentives at play are extremely high, and these athletes may be under tremendous socio-political pressure, as well. Thus, the chances of athletes feeling external pressure to use enhancement substances are significant. In this way, arguably the strongest way to keep this pressure from being more commonplace is to maintain the current prohibition on doping.

In any case, the subtleties of this argument merit closer examination. Firstly, as Tamburrini points out, at least in elite sports, athletes are not in as precarious a position as are construction workers and for this reason, they may have a greater ability to resist pressure. Secondly, at least up to now, the ban on doping has not been able to keep this coercion from taking place. The prohibition has been shown to be ineffective in its ability to protect athletes' interests. So the question at hand is if the lifting of the ban would substantially improve athletes' situation, given that substances would be taken under medical supervision and not just by the people around the athlete. In this way, by making the substances official and providing greater knowledge about the techniques and effects of enhancement through the use of substances or treatments, athletes' autonomy could be bolstered, especially when faced with potential external pressure. A lifting of the doping ban along with the establishment of external and independent medical supervision could bring about more appropriate protection to the health of athletes.

Harm to Others

For some advocates of the ban, doping is not only harmful to the athletes themselves, but it also produces harm to others (Ramos Goridllo 1999; 11). This statement can be interpreted in several different ways. Firstly, by doping, athletes are harming their teammates and rivals who practice the same sport as well as those whom they may compete against. In effect, athletes who dope are coercing their teammates to do the same. This is what is called the "coercion argument."

Secondly, it may harm society in two different ways by affecting youth and promoting doping in other categories of sport and people who play sports at the non-professional level, i.e., amateur and junior athletes.

The Coercion Argument

It is well known that the distinguishing feature of highly competitive sport is the extreme degree of competitiveness of the participating athletes. For this reason, it is not surprising that one athlete's use of these doping substances may drive others to take them, too, so as not to lose the competitive edge.

However, to speak of coercion in these cases seems exaggerated. Athletes who are reticent to dope could feel pressured to emulate those others who have not very prudently decided to take those substances, but nothing impedes them from opposing this pressure. Those athletes will have fewer chances to become "winners." In principle, it does not seem objectionable that we accept the fact that there are winners and losers as an essential element to the practice of sport, i.e., not all the participants in a competition are to be treated equally. Consideration should be taken to honor those athletes who have made the extra effort or who have taken risky decisions.

But this does not seem to pose a significant moral problem. An analogy could be made using the case of war correspondents. An ambitious war correspondent puts his or her life at risk to obtain exclusive news footage or spectacular photos, and thanks to that success, the journalist is rewarded. Is this individual not indirectly challenging colleagues to do the same? Should risky behavior that leads journalists to put their lives in danger be prohibited so that other war correspondents do not feel that same pressure? It seems that the answer to this is no. Well-informed adults have the right to decide for themselves what risks to take in their professional lives as long as others are not harmed by this decision. There is no reason to treat athletes any differently.

Tamburrini concludes with a recommendation that all other circumstances being unchanged, if an athlete puts his/her life at risk to obtain a victory, while others are more prudent, there is nothing more fair than giving the prize to the risk taker.

Athletes as Models

A common objection to permitting doping is that star athletes act as role models for young people. Following this line of thought, without the prohibition, athletes would probably be emulated in their doping habits by young people, leading to an increase in the consumption of drugs and doping substances among youth. Studies carried out in the 1980s in the United States indicate that approximately one million American youth abuse steroids. And this fact would bring about considerable social damage. For this reason the authors maintain that because athletes serve as role models for young people, they have a moral duty in the dangerous activity of consuming doping substances.

The first part of this objection assumes that the performance-enhancing methods (including doping substances) can be treated the same as recreational drugs. However, I shall follow Tamburrini's line of thought in pointing out that making doping tantamount to the consumption of recreational drugs is based on confusion; it is wrong to say that doping and recreational drugs are the same, as this objection appears to do. In the first place, it is an error because doping substances and treatments may negatively affect an athlete's health, but they do not tend to be addictive. Secondly, whatever sacrifices an athlete makes to attain better performance, the chance to win would be put at risk if drugs were taken. Sports are incompatible with drugs. Following this interpretation, Tamburrini coined the phrase "sports should be clean" in keeping with the idea of leading a healthy life. If individuals want to take on physical activity, whether it be professional or amateur, then they have to lead an appropriate lifestyle (Tamburrini 2000b; 18).

This objection can be understood another way: it may be possible that young people are tolerant of doping practices and they also know that their sport idols take these substances. In this way, damaging messages with regard to the value of effort and sacrifice are conveyed.

An appropriate response to this objection would be to point out that it is certain that successful athletes are social role models, but so are their parents; no one has proposed punishing parents who smoke or drink in front of their children. The social harm caused by tobacco and alcohol use in children is likely greater than the damaging effects that may be provoked by young athletes doping without medical supervision.

In addition to the concern for children's and young athletes' physical health, there would be a certain incongruence in allowing rigorous training programs, which are often more damaging to young athletes. How do we know that these injuries are lesser than those caused by doping? It seems fairly clear that at least some doping methods are innocuous, such as caffeine and blood doping.

Doping and the Rules of Sports

One widespread objection to athletes' use of performance-enhancing substances is that they go against the nature of sporting competitions. The underlying idea is that doping ought to be prohibited because it is, in some way, not ethical and against the true nature of sport (Schneider and Butcher 2000; 14).

The argument that is presented here is especially interesting because this objection is being raised to the use of doping within the framework of sport without necessarily denying that the use of these substances may be valid outside the scope of sport. Tännsjö has pointed out that medical interventions are viewed very differently in general medicine than in sports medicine. At first glance it seems more feasible to carry out risky medical interventions within the sports arena, i.e., there is a greater tolerance for risk taking, given the fact that athletes tend to accept the uncertainty of results due to their interest in returning to their sport as soon as possible (Tännsjö 2009; 19).

However, in some way there can be specific reasons in the field of sport that make it impossible for a certain type of medical intervention to be carried out, especially those that aim to enhance athletic performance. This is because the current rules that govern the practice of sport are those that appeal to certain values inherent to sport, values which would be put in danger if this type of intervention were allowed (Moller 2010; 115).

Tamburrini calls this objection "the essentialist argument" perhaps precisely because of Sandel's book chapter dealing with sport called "The Essence of the Game."

Inside this generic "nature of sport" category, there are in reality several different objections. In this section I will highlight some of them based on Tamburrini's observations:

1. Doping will eliminate components of uncertainty and excitement from sport.
2. With doping it would be unnecessary for athletes to put forth effort or make sacrifice to obtain good results in sport.
3. The loss of spirit in the practice of sport.
4. The loss of popularity of sport.
5. Doping would eliminate or reduce the human element of sport.

Doping and the Elimination of the Emotional Content of Sport

Regarding the first argument, the supporters of the ban on enhancement claim that doping removes the element of excitement from sport because the results would be more predictable. The argument states that instead of being a dispute between individuals, competition would be turned into a struggle between bodies that are enhanced through the use of technology (Tamburrini 2000b), thus making the result more predictable due to the technological improvements of the athletes.

In a certain sense, the state of sport, at least in certain more characteristic disciplines, is based on a competition between athletes (or groups) whose result is predictable. This degree of uncertainty is what provokes the interest of the spectators who want to see something of a struggle or fight between rivals under equal conditions. This aspect is what generates excitement causing the desire to know what the final score will be. Professional sport is to a great extent indebted to this link between unpredictability of the score and excitement, since excitement is a core component for spectators. This interest in the emotion of the game generates the attention of spectators who are eventually willing to compensate athletes for allowing those watching to enjoy the technical abilities but also for allowing them to relish in the excitement of the competition.

The critique based on this loss of emotion cannot be extended to the practice of all sports. The improvement of technical abilities through the use of pharmacological performance-enhancing substances would reduce the uncertainty in some sports, but not in all. Tamburrini highlights that those sports in which the performance is judged within a space-time framework (e.g., in meters, seconds or kilograms) would surely be affected. This is the case of weight lifting, foot races, and field events like jumps or throwing (of weights, javelin, etc.). But there are other disciplines where the main relevant factor for success and triumph or the ability to measure the athlete is the creative element. Think about Messi, the extraordinary soccer player endowed with astonishing speed. However, his greatness as a player is not due to speed (there are players faster than him), but rather to his extraordinary ability to dominate and control the ball while on the run, as well as to his acute sense of the game as a whole. These qualities do not seem to lend themselves to being developed, increased or enhanced with chemical substances or genetic technology. Regarding this type of game where factors other than strictly time-space ones are at play, the influence of doping substances would be much less, and for this reason there would be no corresponding loss in the uncertainty and emotional component of the game.

One variant to this objection is that genetic technology in sport would give way to a situation in which competitions would not be won by the best athletes, but rather by those who were doped to achieve better results in a certain sporting ability.

However, as has been pointed out above, at least in the current state of affairs, no miraculous results or extraordinary athletes can be obtained just by taking a little pill or modifying a gene. Athletes will need to continue training and making sacrifices to be able to attain top marks and, therefore, those athletes who trust in the results delivered by a miracle pill will hardly be among the sporting elite.

Additionally, to reiterate a previous point, there is a certain incoherence in prohibiting doping based on the unfair advantage that it would impart to the athlete, while ignoring measures related to other random factors causing advantages (being born in a wealthy country, or simply being blessed in the genetic lottery and enjoying special athletic abilities).

The Non-Necessity of Athletes' Effort

With regard to this objection, it must be said that what it purports is rather a caricature of the potential impact of doping technologies in the field of sport. As Tamburrini notes, equality would actually be produced as a result of generalizing these treatments, leading to a situation in which effort, dedication, and sacrifice would become much more decisive factors in sport than they are at present. The reason appears to be simple: given that athletes would not differ as much from each other in terms of their physical abilities, victory in competition would depend on excellence of character and not as much on fortune in the genetic lottery.

The Loss of the Spirit of the Practice of Sport

Another objection is that doping would corrupt sport, or it would lose the attractiveness that it currently has, given that the values inherent to the sport, e.g., skill, drama and joy, would be negatively affected. Tamburrini offers the following values as those intrinsic to the "sporting game" (Tamburrini 2000b; 66).

1. Flow: a good game needs to have a certain fluidity that allows differing combinations to unfold and flourish, thus displaying the characteristics of the game itself.
2. Skill: in a good game, participants need to develop a relatively high level of technical mastery.
3. Challenge: a good game should be a competition among rivals. A game among competitors who are not on equal footing is not a good game. Intensity would be lacking and the results could be known ahead of time.
4. Excitement: a good game will have an uncertain outcome with participants having high levels of ability. It is likely then that the game will be exciting.
5. Drama: a good game unfolds where equal conditions and intense competition exist, thus keeping the results unknown and undecided until the last seconds of the game and adding a sense of drama to the competition.
6. Joy: in a good game there is a flow in the game, skills are high, and competition is exciting and among equals. Competitors and spectators alike experience a sense of enjoyment while immersed in a state-of-the-art practice of hedonism.

Examining each of these characteristics in light of doping, the conclusion can be reached that none would be negatively affected by the improvements proffered by athletes' doping. Tamburrini remarks that in terms of flow and skill, the situation would remain unchanged even if athletes took doping substances. It could even be said that certain elements would improve.

Regarding other elements of the game, the balance could also turn in favor of doping. If enhancements are officially controlled and if implementation criteria are established for each sport, it is then likely that competition would become more equal than it currently is given the current predominance of the natural genetic lottery. If greater equality were to exist among athletes, it is likely that greater excitement and drama would follow. In turn, this would cause greater joy in the game. Even though a description of this future cannot be offered with absolute certainty, there is a distinct possibility that these predictions would pan out, given the equal physical conditions that there would be among competitors.

Doping and the Decline of Sport Popularity

Another argument that has been furnished against doping is that it could seriously affect the properties that current sport is founded on, thus causing a decline in sport popularity. It is reasonable to assume that in competitions where athletes regularly use doping techniques, the passion for the sport could fall because fans would not expect as much in terms of physical displays. Viewed from another standpoint, sport would not be especially different from a horse race in which speed and endurance are the most important characteristics of the animals (Savulescu, Foddy, and Clayton 2004).

Nevertheless, this may not be the case, and there are no conclusive reasons offered in the analyzed cases. There are two arguments that could be offered in this regard. First, the current commercialization and professionalization of sport does not seem to have affected its popularity. It could even be said that the opposite has taken place.

Secondly, even those sports where enhancement techniques have been introduced in recent times, thus becoming a main component of competition (as is the case in automobile races), the passion for the sport has not declined; on the contrary, it has increased (Tamburrini 2000b).

Doping and Human Values of Sport

The values examined in the previous section are intrinsic to sport, but it should also be pointed out that these could be seen in other competitions where the participants are not human beings. Let us imagine a chicken fight or a dog race. Both cases demonstrate the characteristics that Tamburrini predicts for sports.

What is it that distinguishes sports from these other competitions? The answer seems simple. Sport is a human activity. And the problem arises when the spread of doping makes sport become mainly a technical activity and less "human." That does not only affect the uncertainty of the final results, it also perverts the essence of the sport itself, which consists of measuring human abilities, not the abilities of pharmacological and genetic research and development on doping substances and techniques. This is Sandel's point of view (Sandel 2007). He sees sport as linked to the natural skills and talents of human ;beings, and doping constitutes an artificial intervention; even though its purpose may be enhancement, it does nothing more than damage the human nature of sport itself.

Several years ago Simon remarked on this threat, claiming that the main element of athletic competition is to prove and establish comparisons between the distinct physical abilities of athletes, not the physical-chemical question consisting in evaluating how organisms react to different drugs (Simon 1995; 212).

It is worthwhile to consider several objections to these arguments. Firstly, Savulescu points out that the decision to take a doping substance is also a human decision (Savulescu, Foddy, and Clayton 2004). It is the choice of an athlete, which for all intents and purposes, is no different from any other decision that impacts on athletic performance: the tactics or strategies to be used during a game or a race, or what type of training to follow. In this way, the decision is more human (since it is taken freely by the athlete) than other aspects of sport successes which are random (some physical abilities are simply inherited).

Secondly, in actual sports there are many technological improvements that have remarkably changed some athletic competitions. For example, the introduction of fiberglass field hockey sticks made the sport somewhat less technical and, at the same time, more dependent on physical strength and speed. This has been highlighted to explain the decline of historically powerful teams, Pakistan and India, against the rise of European teams. A similar situation is seen in pole vaulting with carbon fiber poles. Yet another sport where the advances in technology have changed the way of playing is tennis, where rackets made of new materials in the grips and the strings have allowed tennis players to develop amazingly fast serves, to the detriment of the technical and stylized game that took place several years back. Another greatly controversial case is that of polyurethane swimsuits (Murray 2008).

The question of the impact of technological advances does not stop here. They have not only had deep reverberations on the development of competition, they have also had an impact on the training of athletes. What are known as hyperbaric chambers aid in the oxygenation capacity of athletes, which at the same time increase their endurance. These cases demonstrate a certain contradiction in banning certain substances and treatments.

OTHER PROBLEMS WITH THE DOPING BAN

The Problems of Prosecution

The prosecution of doping has not seen resounding success, a fact which brings about questions regarding its focus and application. But it can, also, generate effects that it purports to avoid, as was the case with the famous "dry law," according to Savulescu.

Savulescu's argument compares the consequences of a doping ban with the famous dry law (Savulescu, Foddy and Clayton 2004, 669). In effect, this thesis is not only that anti-doping controls in general have been a rather considerable failure for not having discouraged the use of doping in athletes, at least in some sports, but that the prohibition of an in-demand substance brings about other intrinsic damages of its own.

To justify such an assertion, Savulescu resorts to the well-known example of regulation of alcohol in the United States during the 1920s. The ban on selling and consuming alcohol led to a change in the drinking habits of Americans and an eventual increase in consumption. Taken out of public view, alcohol began to be consumed within private homes, where it was readily available. This had immediate consequences on the mortality rate due to alcohol. In contrast, the same statistics went down in other countries where there was no prohibition. Additionally, given that alcohol quality was not officially regulated, the physical injuries (and deaths) caused by adulterated alcohol, poisoned or "bad" alcohol actually increased (Savulescu, Foddy and Clayton 2004; 669).

Nevertheless, even if it were the case that prohibition had caused a decrease in consumption, that would have led to the creation of a black market that would meet the needs of those who still wished to consume banned products. By definition, black markets lack regulation, which implies that their use is irregular and the safety of the product when it is consumed by the purchaser is questionable. The most recent notorious case was that of cyclist Riccardo Riccò who nearly died after undergoing a blood transfusion in his own home.

Savulescu adds that the direct risk of prohibiting doping substances and techniques in sport does nothing other than increase the risks mentioned above. Currently, the ban is in effect so that once the decision to take a doping substance (or use a technique) has been made, the amount that corresponds to the desire for a certain physical performance must be chosen. It is easy to imagine that in this stage the athlete could choose a dose that is dangerous to his or her health. If, on the contrary, doping and the corresponding medical supervision (obtaining correct dosage for a certain performance while protecting health) were legally allowed, it would be more likely that the risks inherent to the taking of uncontrolled substances would be avoided (or at least, they would be minimized).

But the advocates of maintaining anti-doping controls could still argue that the efficacy of those controls will continue to improve in the future along with the improvements in the technology use. That is, perfecting the imposition of research and anti-doping controls would be the solution to this problem. However, the prosecution of doping is difficult. Athletes are becoming increasingly subversive by using developed drugs of which the authorities are not yet aware, or by using mechanisms that

hide or mask their consumption. It cannot even be dismissed that undetectable substances may be created. This was the case of Bay Area Laboratory Co-Operative (BALCO), a San Francisco laboratory that made and
distributed a new synthetic steroid. According to the U.S. Anti-Doping
Agency, ten athletes were sanctioned for having tested positive for THG
or a Modafinil-type substances administered by BALCO. Sprinters Kelli
White and Alvin Harrison were also sanctioned after a police investigation demonstrated that there had also been a relationship with the in-
criminated laboratory. Furthermore, the USADA sanctioned other athletes, including the 100-meter world record holder, American Tim Mont-
gomery and sprinters Chryste Gaines and Michelle Collins, for their alleged ties to BALCO. The athlete Marion Jones, a triple champion in the
Sydney Olympic Games, was also implicated in the scandal.

What is interesting about the BALCO case is that the substances provided to the athletes were not discovered in anti-doping tests, since the
tests were shown to be incapable of detecting the substance. The whole
scandal started with an anonymous sample containing the residue of a
new generation steroid that had been, up to that point, undetectable in
tests. It is likely that in spite of all the attempts to eradicate doping, deceit
will still continue and results will continue to be unfair (Douglas 2007).

TECHNICAL DIFFICULTIES

Related to the relative fallibility of anti-doping controls highlighted in the
previous section, it is necessary to record two additional problems: there
can be both false negatives and false positives. In other words, results to
anti-doping tests can deliver a negative result when in fact there was a
case of doping, and on the flip side, they can deliver positive results
where there was truly no consumption of doping substances.

Given the media repercussions that doping cases have on professional
athletes as well as the economic, social and psychological harm derived
from a doping charge, the risk of false positives is especially severe. The
recent case of Marta Domínguez provides an example of those risks that
arise from the technical difficulties to anti-doping tests.

Another case is that of the American basketball player Diana Taurasi,
who played for the Turkish club Fenerbahçe. This club rescinded Taurasi's contract when she tested positive after a league game. Afterwards the
Turkish Basketball Federation team was disqualified from playing in the
Turkish league. Taurasi nevertheless insisted from the outset that she had
not used performance-enhancing drugs.

Some time later, it was proven that there had been a false positive, a
fact that led the club to demand a public apology and the resignation of
the laboratory directors of the Ankara-based lab. Sekip Mosturoglu, a
member of Fenerbahçe's executive board, accused the lab of "inadequa-

cies" and stated that their report about Taurasi's alleged consumption of Modafinil had tainted the reputation of the WNBA star as well as that of the club itself.

The World Anti-Doping Agency, which has the authority to suspend or revoke doping laboratories' accreditation, said that they had requested an explanation for Taurasi's positive Modafinil test. The WADA, which relies on thirty-five accredited laboratories around the world, had previously suspended the Ankara lab for three months in 2009 for non-compliance with international standards.

Another player affected by the same case was the American Monique Coker, who plays for Cyhan Belediyesi and had also had a positive test result for Modafinil in tests by the same laboratory.

Lack of Objective Criteria for the Inclusion of Prohibited Substances and Treatments

There have also been recurring critiques directed at the prohibited substances and treatments list. Several examples demonstrate that the criteria for inclusion/exclusion of substances and treatments are far from being clear and justified.

For example, Erythropoietin (EPO) is a natural hormone that stimulates production of red blood cells, increasing the total cell mass, i.e., the percentage of blood made up of red blood cells (hemoglobin). This factor is important in sport since performance is determined by the ability to carry oxygen to the muscles, and this ability to carry oxygen depends particularly on the red blood cells that are in charge of this transportation: the more red blood cells, the more oxygen can be carried. EPO is produced naturally by the body in response to anemia, hemorrhaging, pregnancy or living at high altitude. For this reason, some athletes train at high altitudes to improve their level of hemoglobin. However, EPO is banned because it increases the number of red blood cells and drives hemoglobin to dangerous, even fatal, levels. EPO was officially prohibited in 1985, after athletes had been taking artificial injections for years.

However, the same EPO results are produced by training at high altitude and more recently through hypoxicator systems. The body responds by segregating EPO naturally and increasing the number of blood cells so that they can absorb more oxygen with each breath. Nonetheless, EPO is prohibited, while hyperbaric chambers are not.

Along the same lines, V. Moller (Moller 2010) points out that products like acetaminophen, which comes in certain types of sprays and injections, is applied on athletes throughout the practice of sport. The aim of this use is clearly the enhancement of physical abilities of the athlete, but these are, nonetheless, permitted.

Additionally, there are authors who question certain substances like caffeine that have been on the list and now are not, even though there are no conclusive studies on its performance-enhancing effects. In effect, caffeine (together with ephedrine and pseudoephedrine) stopped being considered doping substances for the Athens Olympic Games in 2004. But what can be said about those athletes who were sanctioned before that?

In sum, this continues to be a controversial topic in scientific literature: "some studies affirm that the administration of caffeine improves sport performance while others do not" (Gracia Marco et al. 2009; 71)

Psychology of the Athlete and the Prisoner's Dilemma

But it seems that in spite of the sheer quantity of doping tests established and the economic effort put into anti-doping awareness campaigns, using those treatments and substances still seems to be the "order of the day." It appears to be hard to eradicate this habit, given that the will to be better, at any cost, seems to be part of the psychological make-up of the athlete. Because of this idiosyncratic desire to reach goals and gain fame, to be paid large sums of money, or other similar goals, it is highly unlikely that current or future forms of doping would absolutely disappear. What is more, in terms of doping, athletes are faced with a so-called "prisoner's dilemma."

Several authors (Haugen 2004, Breivik 1992) have put forward this notion of the dilemma regarding doping. This theoretical model shows that when the possibility of being discovered is low and the rewards for winning are high, it is predicted that athletes have great incentives to cheat. The current situation faced by athletes encourages doping, even knowing that they are worse off if everyone takes doping treatments or substances than if no one does.

Take, for example, the situation represented in the matrix in which two athletes, A and B, have the choice to dope or not, but neither knows if the other will actually do so and neither can they communicate with each other. On the other hand, they do know the rewards that are derived from their possible choices: to dope or not to dope. Both are equally motivated to win a contest.

In this matrix, the best results would be those of 4 and 1. The first number in the cells represents A's preference and the second number B's.

A has two options, to dope or not. Given that the reward is great to not dope, 4, he would choose this option. In B's counterpart situation, he would therefore choose to dope. If both were to use the same strategy

		B	
		No Doping	Doping
A	No Doping	3.3	1.4
	Doping	4.1	2.2

with the hope of obtaining the best result, then both players would collapse in the cell (2,2).

If A decided not to dope in hopes that B did the same, the best collective result would be obtained (3,3), but A runs the risk of being "exploited" by B who could choose not to dope and in so doing A would obtain the worst reward (1) and B would get the best (4).

B's line of thought would be analogous. That is, the fear of being exploited by the other prevents him from arriving at the best collective result: cell (3,3). As a result, the dominant strategy for both is to dope, but this is not the best collective result, even though they could avoid being exploited by each other.

The "prisoner's dilemma" demonstrates the need to cooperate (both athletes would be better off if they cooperated with each other and did not engage in doping), and, at the same time, it shows that under certain conditions, the athlete's rational choice to protect his or her own interest fatally leads to an inadequate balance. In other words, this result is worse than the other possibilities for both parties, an effect that is not desirable at all.

The current mechanism for avoiding this undesirable result for all the parties involved in the "prisoner's dilemma" is threatening sanctions, with which it is hoped that athletes do not choose doping. The issue is that if tests are not completely effective and the rewards obtained by athletes who engage in doping are high, the incentives to continue with this practice are high. Domestic and international authorities are continuing to work for improved testing and to impose harsher sanctions. Even so, it seems that the fight against doping is still fraught with difficulties, or in the opinion of others, it is a resounding failure.

CONCLUSIONS

In light of these arguments, it would then seem to be a reasonable alternative to lift the ban on doping and simultaneously establish a regulatory framework where the consumption of performance-enhancing substances were medically supervised, making available conditions of equality for all the participants. In this way, the main goal—protecting athletes' health—of this anti-doping struggle would be better met. Consumption would be allowed so that athletes' health was not harmed, and at the same time the negative effects of clandestine doping would be avoided.

Additionally, I have attempted to show that the other two arguments used in the anti-doping fight are not justified: the effect on equality among athletes is not greater when doping is permitted than with other aspects of sport, and the "spirit of sport" is not violated or dehumanized. Taking doping substances is a decision that athletes make, as they do with any other strategy, diet, or training system that is designed to improve their results. All of these choices would benefit the athlete's ability to choose the best means to set personal bests. And with that, the practice of sport has absolutely no reason to lose either excitement or popularity.

THREE

Sport and Sexual Discrimination

The world of sport has historically been one of men; one where women did not enter. For an overview of this situation, take the narrative of Greek historian Pausanias which recounts that in classic Greece one directive commanded that women who observed the Olympic Games, where obviously only men participated, be thrown over the cliffs. More recently, the exclusion of women from the first modern Olympics was justified by Coubertin in that women were not prepared for sport (Schneider 2000). In this way, sport constituted one of the first arenas where discrimination faced by women was more evident. And yet, despite women's bursting onto the sporting scene in recent years, their participation in terms of sheer numbers and results obtained is far from being comparable to that of men. In addition, the sport environment is one of the few where sexual discrimination continues, given that most competitions are segregated: men compete with men and women with women, whether or not women have athletic abilities that are equal or better than that of their male counterparts. And few voices are raised among spectators, sporting authorities or by the athletes themselves to cry out against this situation, especially in the flagrant cases where women have demonstrated equal abilities to those of men, as in the case of archery (and other sports based on precision), motor sports, golf, billiards, equestrian competitions, sailing, chess, etc.

Awareness of these problems of inequality that women face as compared to the dominant male group has risen with the passage of time. The core discussion has revolved around the situation of women, but recently the discussion about equality has been expanded in order to deal with problems that had always been present, but which have increased in recent times. This is the case of transsexual and hermaphrodite athletes, as in the famous case of the South African runner Caster Semenya, whose

53

physiology has a chromosomal anomaly, and not having ovaries but internal testicles, it is difficult to categorize her as male or female for sporting competitions. I will return to this question later on.

But historically, there have been two predominate issues regarding the role of women in sport: exclusion of women in sport and the proposed norms for equalization. The first of these topics is descriptive, narrating the situation of subordination and stigma in sport that women have suffered. In effect, even in current times, when female athletes set new records, no matter that they are as excellent or worthy of mention as men's, women do not receive the same praise or attention from the media, nor do they receive the same economic compensation. The second topic, regarding sports and sex in terms of the rules, has dealt with measures that should be adopted to overcome this inequality. That is, what ways could women obtain equality of opportunity within the scope of sport, especially because sports have been historically designed according to predominately male physical characteristics.

The Exclusion of Women from Sport

Regarding this first topic, feminist authors have described the way women's identity has been constructed both individually and socially based on the body and how sport has intervened in this process, in this traditionally male-dominated area. In terms of sport and the feminine identity, one of the areas that has been stressed is the mechanisms for exclusion of women from sport. For this, I. M. Young (Young 1995) has argued that women have been excluded from the sport arena for two reasons: conceptual and institutional. According to the conceptual justification, women have been historically and culturally defined as static, as bodies and objects in such a way that they did not meet the conditions necessary for sport, which is characterized as an eminently dynamic and active phenomenon. For this reason, it is not surprising that women ended up adopting very masculine values in the field of sport (but in other fields as well):

> As women's sports has become controlled by men it increasingly reflects the most valued characteristic of men's sports: hierarchy, competitiveness and aggression (Dworkin and Messner 2002; 20).

Based on the dominant institutional structures, women have historically had fewer opportunities to explore and improve their athletic potential. However, there has been a change in this situation in current times where it seems to be shifting positively in favor of women's interests.

From a sociological perspective, the nineteenth century influenced the construction of modern sport, based on specifically masculine characters, abilities and strengths:

Rather than breaking down the conventional concept of masculinity and feminity, organized sport has overblown the cultural hegemony of heterosexualized, aggressive, violent, heavily muscled male athletes and heterosexualized, flirtatious, moderately muscled female athletes who are accomplished and competitive but expected to be submissive to the control of men coaches and managers (Dworkin and Messner 2002; 24).

Hans Bonde highlighted that with the onset of the Industrial Revolution, the division in the home between men and women was accentuated so that women became housewives, while men devoted themselves to paying jobs. At that time a series of values and attitudes predominated, and based on these masculine stereotypes they continued to be forged. Thus, according to Bonde, sport consisted of a social domain in which the construction of masculinity was especially important. The socialization of men was carried out based on these values which sport tended to generate and reinforce: individualism, independence, bravery, discipline and a fighting spirit. In this way, with the practice of sport, a man could shape himself, especially his body, according to the potentialities and abilities that were nothing other than a reflection of the society in which he lived. Thus, according to Bonde, speed became the main criterion in the masculine movement of nineteenth-century sport culture (Bonde 1996; 21).

Another aspect that was added to speed as a core trait of sport was technology. As Puig and Mosquera pointed out:

The importance of the technology during the industrial process had effects in the sport, and the young bourgeoisie devised all types of instruments that helped the improvement of the sport performance. They attempted, with the minimum strength, to achieve the maximum efficiency thanks to the technological support (Puig and Mosquera 1998; 167).

Almost simultaneously another ideal about the male body was being put together based on the sporting practices of the working class. Instead of speed, strength was the most important ideal for this group. From this idea boxing clubs, weightlifting, etc., came about among these collectives because workers in this way found a space where they were able to foster group solidarity, an important concept in reclaiming their social rights (Bonde 1996; 23).

Feminist literature has made harsh criticism regarding the attribution of masculine and feminine characteristics and, along with that, the adaptation or lack of adaptation to allow participation in (or not, which is really what interests us here) certain professional sports is not the natural state of affairs, but rather a convention. In this sense, it has been common to distinguish between two concepts: sex and gender. Sex is understood as the biological characteristics of each person which allows him or her to be categorized as male or female. Alternatively, gender is based on social

roles that have been constructed based on biological differences. Therefore, reference is made to social constructions that highlight behaviour,
values, and attitudes which lead to distinguishing between men and
women. With this distinction, scholars have attempted to show that there
is no logical connection between biology and the attribution of social
roles. Women do not necessarily have to overcome any hurdles in order
to take on roles (or models) other than the ones that historically and
socially have been imposed on them in this male-dominated society. It is
effectively the case that both in our current societies as well as in the past,
social stereotypes linked to men have prevailed. Masculine values have
had and continue to have greater social prestige than feminine ones,
while stereotypes associated with women have been viewed as subordinate and inferior (Puig and Mosquera 1998). As a result, Tamburrini and
Tännsjö (2006; 208) are right. This description can be perfectly extrapolat-
ed to the world of sport, where in spite of the transformations that have
taken place over recent decades, inequality between men and women
continues to exist; there is still a valid link between masculinity and
sport. In effect, sport continues to sing the praises of primordial masculine values: competitiveness, success, the desire to stand out and be the
best, physical strength, etc. As Puig and Mosquera highlight, the meaning of competition is not particularly attractive to women, who tend to
choose activities that are more closely linked to the guidelines and values
that they have acquired through the process of socialization.

Fortunately, currently there is a massive influx of women in sport, and
among women there can also be seen a rupture with traditional stereotypes, especially in sports' assumption of competition. However, some
feminists have still pointed out that this influx into (masculine) sport has
not been carried out with a critical eye, the result being that women have
taken up an inferior position in masculine hegemony:

> As girls and women push for equity in sports, they are moving—often
> uncritically—into a hierarchical system that has as its main goal to
> produce winners, champions, and profits (Dworkin and Messner 2002;
> 20).

But still it is not uncommon to find normative arguments that justify
continuing this situation: 1) the argument on the defeminization; 2) the
argument for traditional feminine roles; 3) the argument for protection of
health; and 4) the argument based on competitiveness.

Concerning the first argument, it has been pointed out that sport leads
to, among other things, the defeminization of women, given that physical
exercise contributes to an increase in muscle mass and a loss of beauty.
This argument, if it can even be deemed an argument, reeks of clearly
unjustified male chauvinism and paternalism and deserves little or no
attention or consideration.

The aim of the second argument has been to point out that sports, especially competitive sports, contains demands that are far removed from traditional feminine roles, above all maternal roles. Therefore, it concludes that female athletes experience a sense of contradiction between the traditional stereotype as such and the demands of the practice of sport itself, which obviously present traits that are not (or not very) feminine. While this argument is more sophisticated than the last one, it still fails due to unjustified paternalism. It is women themselves who should decide what social roles they would like to take on, independent of the fact that they are not (very) feminine. Additionally, from an empirical perspective, the objection to female participation in sport is also weak, since numerous sociological studies have made it patently clear that female athletes are comfortable with the sports they practice and they do not suffer any internal conflict of interest in this regard.

The next arguments dealing with protection of health and with competition deserve greater attention. They are strategies that currently show no obvious bias for banning women from sport, but they advocate for segregated competitions for women and men.

Regarding the first argument for male-female segregation in sports like boxing, rugby, soccer and contact sports in general, this argument may be justified on most occasions due to the fact that men's greater physical size and force would probably make women suffer blows and collisions which would then produce severe physical damage. Of course, this reason does not apply to the possibility that the sport is not practiced amongst themselves, but given the relative physical equality between women, injuries would be less likely. However, this continues to be a paternalistic argument that treats woman as beings incapable of making decisions for themselves, even if these decisions lead them to suffer harm. It is a limitation on personal freedom that is difficult to justify and which is not exactly present in other aspects of social life, where women take on professions, carry out tasks and leisure activities, or simply have habits (e.g., smoking) that also pose a danger to their health. The fact that this argument still maintains a marked chauvinist bias is shown in that if the risk of harm were not produced by men, but rather by other external factors or women themselves, it is possible that no one would defend it publicly.

The fourth argument affects one of the internal values of sport: the (relative) equality and competitiveness that should be found among the participants in a sport competition. While it is clear that there are sports in which women obtain similar and sometimes superior marks than men, it is also true that in other sports this is not the case. The general physiological advantages that men enjoy over women in speed, body type, muscle mass, or height consequently lead to an evident superiority in sports over women in many disciplines. This situation is what motivates the existence of separate competitions for men and women, given the fact that not establishing them would entail the disappearance of the value of competitiveness among participants. Likewise, the tension and excitement that are linked to athletic competitions would disappear, especially at the elite level. The argument for sexual segregation is remarkably similar to the arguments used to establish segregated competitions based on weight or level of experience. In the same way, it seems justified that segregated sporting disciplines (in certain justified cases) exist based on sex, even though this justification is more for preserving competition. It goes without saying that this segregation has no reason to be seen in all disciplines, nor do they need to be definitive. Rather, they can be open to the possibility that women obtain similar results to those of men, thus making it feasible to eliminate segregation. Related to this is the proposal that an individual woman (or maybe even a team) who reaches the performance standards of men may be allowed to participate in their competitions. This measure would impede a situation similar to that of the fourteen-year-old Chinese shooter Zhang Shan. This athlete, in spite of her age, became the first woman to win the mixed competition of skeet shooting, and in so doing even set an Olympic record. Even so, a short time later, the Olympic authorities removed skeet shooting from the Olympic trials. Several years ago, coinciding with the Sydney Olympics, the competition was re-introduced, but this time it was segregated.

Nevertheless, it is still true that women have not overcome the general masculine domination of sport, especially because many of the sporting competitions have been shaped using a predominantly masculine framework in such a way that sporting disciplines with more social repercussions and greater popularity within communications media are those that favor typically masculine traits. It is this situation that has led to proposing equalization of men and women in sport. In what follows, I will examine three such proposals: that of Jane English who promotes establishing segregated sports for men and women; that of Tännsjö who favors men and women competing together in all sporting disciplines on equal footing; and lastly, that of Tamburrini who defends an "equality of sexes" policy.

The Normative Conceptions on Equalization

Given the disadvantaged situation of women compared to that of men in sport, several proposals have arisen to overcome this situation of subordination in regard to the masculine dominance of sport. As will be see below, several authors question the current situation in which the majority of disciplines are strictly separated by sex. As has been highlighted in other sectors of society, the sport environment is considered to be intrinsically sexist because it responds to conceptions of the body, personal relationships and even morality that are characteristic of men, and not of women. Given that most disciplines were created and designed by men, on few occasions do women obtain marks or scores that are equal or better than those of men. This situation is considered prejudicial for women because it means that they cannot receive the assets generated by elite sport: fame and economic compensation in addition to an important boost in self-esteem. As long as this situation is perpetuated, women will not have opportunities in the future to be on equal footing with men. For this reason, just as has happened in other social arenas, equalization proposals have been made that aim to overcome historical and underlying discrimination in athletic competitions.

The Establishment of Segregated Sports for Women and for Men

Jane English suggests distinguishing two sport arenas, which can be summarized with the terms "recreational" and "professional" (English 1995). Regarding the former, given that the goods that this arena provides are basic (health, fun, sense of cooperation, a critical sense, a sense of one's own limits, etc.), she proposes that feminine sports be the object of a positive discrimination treatment, so that women have equal opportunity to enjoy the basic benefits of sport.

On the other hand, what characterizes professional sport is that success in them is associated with scarce resources: fame and fortune. Regarding professional sports, English suggests that the distribution criteria should not be those that are in force currently: the results and the preferences of spectators. In effect, sporting disciplines provide athletes with social prestige, fame, and great economic resources causing greater fervour among spectators. These spectators are the ones who are willing to pay for tickets to go to stadiums and to pay for pay-per-view broadcasts on television, money that later serves to reward athletes. Of course, the distribution criteria are mainly based on obtaining great times and good results.

The alternative suggested by English proposes that woman compete in sporting disciplines where they would suffer no actual physiological disadvantage to men, since the disciplines created would be created paying attention to masculine physiological features. When women participate in such sport, they start out at a disadvantage and it is difficult (or at least improbable) to attain the same results as men. Faced with this situation, it would be desirable to create alternative sporting disciplines which are designed with the skills and abilities that are innate to women and reward them equally. In other words, segregated groups by sex would be established; there would be sports reserved exclusively for men and others for women. The foundation for this strategy would be that women in this way would be able to obtain their fair share of the scarce benefits that are derived from sport, especially glory and economic recompense.

Several objections have been directed at this type of measure. In the first place, the inverse of the phenomenon predicted by English could actually occur. Thus such sports would not enjoy massive or majority social support. Additionally, social hostility could be generated against the women who practice them. That is, a certain rejection towards exclusively female competitions could be produced instead of egalitarian integration of women in sport. It would not be unthinkable that these opposite effects were produced instead of those predicted by these measures, given that they may stigmatize the favored group, seeing them as inferior or incapable of reaching their goals on their own. As Tamburrini points out, granting similar recognition and prizes to women who have not actually met the same standards of sport success could be interpreted by the public as unjustified interference with market mechanisms (Tamburrini 2000; 158).

A more powerful objection to English's proposal is based on the fact that these new measures would discriminate against men who may actually be able to achieve superior athletic results in these new trials reserved for women, but they would be kept from participating. This is the meritocratic argument.

Nevertheless, several responses have been brandished in the face of this critique. Firstly, in terms of generating hostility or resentment, it is nevertheless true even if fans are resentful that positive discrimination measures in order to bolster equality still deliver results in terms of increased fairness.

Secondly, it is nothing more than conjecture to point to the fact that hostility toward the favored social group might be produced. In other social arenas, measures of reverse discrimination have not provoked such reactions; in any case, they need to be examined on a case-by-case basis.

In response to the meritocratic argument, a possible answer could take into account the fact that there is actually no one unique concept of equality. In other words, equality does not only have to be observed at the end (or output) of the treatment cycle. That is, if it is observed that the allocation of goods come from justice, one conception of equality would be that all individuals should be placed in the same output line, and that the "best" obtain the goods to be divvied up. The critique to this objection is that precisely the objective that is sought after with reverse discrimination measures is that of overcoming the severe inequalities that may have previously affected women and further obtaining more just relationships between men and women in sport. Said another way, the measures attempt to make formal equality compatible with substantial equality. In conclusion, the reply to the meritocratic argument is that these discriminatory measures are justified by the integration of women in sport and by the increase in self-respect that they would enjoy thanks to segregated sporting disciplines where they could become "better sportspeople in absolute terms." In this way, they would earn self-respect and they could become social idols as are men in "their sporting disciplines."

However, when the feminist replies seem correct from a fairness point of view, I think that the next valid "realist" objection is relevant. Tamburrini indicates that there is an assumption in English's argument that such new women-only sporting practices would catch public attention so that a market for the scarce goods would be formed, just as has happened with sports dominated by men (soccer, basketball, etc.). The matter at hand is that it is impossible to say who should decide this; there is nothing up to now that allows us to deduce what will generate this interest in new women-only sporting competitions.

Extreme Equalization between Men and Women

A provocative position regarding equality between men and women in sport has been proposed by Torbjörn Tännsjö. Just as other authors have put forward the idea of "sexually neutral law" as a measure of equality between men and women, in order to do away with discrimination in sport once and for all, Tännsjö proposes that men and women compete against each other. In the same way, there are other areas of life in which barriers to discrimination have been knocked down and sport should be no exception. In this way, impartiality in terms of sex would be honored:

> The reasons for giving up sexual discrimination within sports, and for allowing individuals of both sexes to compete with each other, is simple. In sports it is crucial that the best person wins. Then sexual differences are simply irrelevant. If a female athlete can perform better than a male athlete, this female athlete should be allowed to compete with, and beat, the male athlete. If she cannot beat a certain male athlete, so be it. If the competition was fair, she should be able to face the fact that he was more talented. It is really simple as that (Tännsjö 2007; 347).

However, these extreme egalitarian measures are tantamount to those generated by legal norms that ignore the sex of the intended audience. It happens that in spite of being formally egalitarian, they tend to maintain existing discrimination. Such egalitarian measures generate what has been called indirect discrimination. This occurs, for example, in the setting of standards for entrance into the police force; the same physical standard is required for both sexes (a height of 1.65 cm.). While most men are taller than this, fewer women supersede this height. In other words, extreme equality would lead to the marginalization of women. In sport, these neutral competitions would contribute to maintaining existing discrimination and would additionally affect the self-respect of athletes.

In the same sense, Tamburrini has objected to Tannsjö's proposal since it does not contribute to eliminating or reducing the disadvantaged situation of women in sport because it treats both sexes equally. It may still be a reasonable policy, but treating both those who are equal and those who are not (women) inevitably involves widening the gap in inequality while at the same time perpetuating it in time (Tamburrini 2000; 160).

Equally critical is Schneider who condemns the Swedish author's proposal as utopian given that in current society women are not actually accorded respect equal to that of men. Rather, women live in a context where they do not reach positions of power or even public relevance. These social circumstances are completely opposite of those of the world of men. For this reason Tännsjö's proposal is currently impractical:

> I assume that perhaps like in Plato's Republic, he wishes that women could play their full roles in all aspects of human life and endeavor. I assume that Tännsjö's vision of philosophical purity momentarily clouded his perception and knowledge of the world we actually live. Other things being equal, I'm not sure the picture he paints would be good. But other things are not equal (Schneider 2000; 137).

The Position of Gender Equity in Sport

The discussion regarding appropriate measure to eliminate discrimination against women in sport is not exhausted by the proposals in the two previous sections. An alternative proposal is put forward by Tamburrini, a position I find defensible with a slight modification that I will highlight at the end.

The program of sexual equalization measures in sport that Tamburrini lays out differs in three ways: 1) the short-term and long-term measures; 2) measures to be adopted within the sport arena and outside of it; and 3) measures to be adopted in elite sport and in childhood and youth sport.

Regarding the first point, Tamburrini highlights that the ultimate goal of his gender equity program is for all the current segregation based on physiological differences between men and women to disappear. He basically posits that feminists have been taking part in sporting disciplines that have constructing based on masculine skills, thus leading to discrimination against women. This outlook is unfair and therefore, a gender equity program aspires to an egalitarian panorama.

Notwithstanding, Tamburrini is realistic and aware that currently physiological differences are quite marked in some sports, and that the suppression of segregation would likely have more negative consequences than positive ones for women since their potential minor sport achievements could affect their self-esteem.

However, in this general framework, the Argentine author establishes two proposals. The first is regarding those who perform exceptionally well in sport and obtain results similar to those of men. Here there is no justification to stop them from participating on equal footing. This is the case of the Chinese shooter Zhang Shan who Tamburrini gives as an example. Or the Chinese swimmer, Ye Shien, who at sixteen-years-old could perfectly compete with her male counterparts, including the Olympic champion Ryan Lochte. The second suggestion that he makes is somewhat more risky. It implies taking immediate action consisting of placing a percentage of women on sports teams. It is well known that some sports have mixed teams of men and women, as is the case of tennis. For Tamburrini there is the potential in team sport to exploit the respect for equality between men and women, and for that reason he suggests, for example, making soccer teams made up of half women and half men. In this way, the confidence of female athletes will increase, as well as their self-respect. The other advantage is that mixed-sex teams "might have the effect of making men and women share the rewards of money and public recognition, stemming from a victory on more fair terms than at present. This, in my opinion, is not a bad beginning" (Tamburrini 2000; 165).

Another aspect that Tamburrini's proposal considers is distinguishing among the measures for sexual integration in society and in the field of sport. Here, it deals with finding a justification for a policy as equally radical as that of Tännsjö. And his answer, as has been mentioned above, consists of highlighting that women have not attained the same results as men in sport, and adopting extreme equalization measures could be counterproductive to the interests of the female athletes themselves. Therefore, the gender equality program he proposes is progressive, allowing temporary segregation in some disciplines until comparable results are attained between men and women.

Thirdly, Tamburrini asserts that equality in participation of men and women in sport should take place starting in childhood and youth. The reasons for this are twofold. The first is empirically based: there are few physiological differences between boys and girls at this age. The second reason is normative: the social and sport role models that they would be exposed to would be the same for both girls and boys, and it is hoped that this would continue into adulthood.

The final proposal that Tamburrini makes for the equalization between sexes in sport are typical measures of reverse discrimination: a) promoting disciplines that favor innately female physical skills; b) introducing a new set of sporting disciplines that are adapted to the physiology of women; and c) assigning greater reward and public recognition to female athletes.

In general terms, Tamburrini's proposal is convincing in that it attempts to combine idealist and realistic measures, and with those measures he lays out a timeline that is not abrupt and thus has the possibility to have predictable positive results in the long term. In particular, the radical proposal of equalization starting in childhood seems well justified, as well as the possibility for women to compete on equal footing in male competitions. I also coincide with the Argentine author regarding the measures of reverse discrimination.

Nevertheless, I do not know to what point the objections raised to English's and Tännsjö's measures are not also applicable to Tamburrini's proposals, since he had previously been criticized for interfering with market preferences. The question is if his last proposal reassigning economic preferences to female athletes is not also an instance of market interference. In my opinion, it is a justifiable measure since the positions that the reverse discrimination measures defend are worthwhile, but I am not so sure that they are coherent within the framework that Tamburrini proposes.

Finally, his proposal on mixed-sex teams could be criticized from the standpoint that it favors safeguarding athletes' health. Following this line of reasoning it may be acceptable to implement such measures in contact sports where there is a certain risk of collisions between players. Nevertheless, as I have previously shown, this is a position of unjustified paternalism: women should be free to run the same risks that men do. However, another problem may crop up: what should be done with men who refuse to play on mixed-sex teams with women? Let us imagine that a federation proposed creating a rugby league with men and women on the same team, but the men refused to play. Should greater weight be given to women's claim to equality or to men's autonomy?

THE CASE OF TRANSEXUALS AND HERMAPHRODITES IN SPORT

As I have highlighted previously, regarding questions of sexual discrimination in sport, questions have arisen on how transexual and hermaphrodite athletes should be treated.

Hermaphrodites

The most famous and controversial case that has arisen is that of the South African athlete Caster Semenya, whose physiology has a chromosomal anomaly rendering her a hermaphrodite since she does not have a uterus or ovaries, but she does have internal testicles. This makes categorizing her as male or female for the purposes of sport problematic. Nevertheless, there have supposedly been cases similar to that of Semenya in the past. Skirstad cites the notorious case of Stella Walsh, a Polish immigrant who lived in the United States and won the gold medal in 1932 for the 100-meter dash under the name Stanislawa Walasiewicz (Skirstad 2000). Some time later, she was actually shot to death while she was doing her shopping at a supermarket. The autopsy revealed that she had both masculine and feminine genitals.

Hermaphroditism is, in biological terms, a characteristic of a living being who possesses reproductive organs of both sexes: male and female.

Therefore, a hermaphrodite has mixed organs capable of producing masculine and feminine gametes.

The debate on the legitimacy of Caster Semenya's participation in athletic competitions arose after winning the 2009 World Track and Field Championship in Berlin at eighteen years of age. Other athletes raised doubts about Semenya's sex before the International Association of Athletics Federations (IAAF), which finally required a sex verification test be performed a few days after Semenya won the medal. To justify this measure, it pointed to the fact that levels of testosterone three times the norm were found in tests in South Africa prior to the World Championship. The tests prior to the Championship were carried out without Semenya's knowledge. Later tests included the chromosome analysis and a gynecological exam. For a number of months, the medal obtained by Caster Semenya was under discussion, provoking a wave of protests in South Africa against the possibility of removing the medal, but also for the public humiliation caused by submitting her to genetic tests that put her femininity in question. For example, the former first lady Winnie Mandela said, "no one had the right to perform tests on 'our little girl,'" and she called for greater patriotism in the South African media in support of the athlete. The president of the Athletics South Africa threatened that "you can' t say somebody's child is not a girl. You denounce my child as a boy when she's a girl? If you did that to my child, I'd shoot you" (Oliver 2010; 75).

In November 2009, the South African Ministry of Sports issued a statement that Semenya had reached an agreement with the IAAF to retain her medal and prize money. The ministry did not indicate whether she would be allowed to compete again as a woman, but it did remark that that IAAF conditions for allowing a person to compete in the athletic competition were not clear. Under these circumstances, a committee of experts was named and tasked with pronouncing the sex of Caster Semenya. Finally in July 2010, an international group of medical experts concluded that Semenya could compete as a women without any limitations.

Nevertheless, the suspicion (or accusation) of hermaphroditism in certain people is a moral problem in itself for two reasons. The first is that the solution that is offered by science regarding the determination of the sex of an individual is not conclusive. The characterization of genes, hormones and genitals is not as simple a task as it would appear to be, since there is not one simple way of classifying men and women. Biology does not place them in stagnate categories of 100 percent man or woman. They are gradual categories.

But this is precisely the result that a simplistic gene test would give. One thing is to observe genes, hormones, and gonads from a purely scientific point of view, and another is to classify an individual as a man or woman, which are not biological categories, but ones which also rely on psychological tendencies, education received and social standards that have been acquired. This is the point that Schneider emphatically makes:

> What makes a woman a woman? Is it chromosomes, genitalia, a way of life or set of roles, or a medical record? It is not clear why medical evidence of surgery and psychology should outweigh chromosomal evidence. In fact it is not clear why any one criterion should be taken as categorically overriding any other (Schneider 2000; 131).

Secondly, the current use of genetics is controversial in determining sex as it pertains to sport, beyond the particular cases in which tests have been carried out without informed consent thus violating patients' rights. The matter at hand is that it is difficult for those tests to account for the complexity of sexual development disorders. On top of that, they can stigmatize the athlete and provoke emotional trauma on the individuals who are subjected to them, especially if the results are positive (Wonkam, Fieggen, and Ramesar 2010; 546). Even though body inspections are no longer carried out, as they were habitually done until the 1970s, having sexual identity tests performed still implies traumatic effects due to the doubts that they generate. Faced with the possibility of having to submit to genetic tests, the number of athletes who have removed themselves from athletic events before they start is not insignificant. Curiously, the practice of genetic tests has been decreasing due to the confluence of two factors: the economic impact that carrying out these tests involves together with the considerable rise in women participating in sport.

The question that the Semenya case puts on the table is how to classify these individuals: as males or females? In the world of sport, several reasons point to the reasons why this topic is by no means trivial. Firstly, because the inclusion of female athletes among males assumes that their performance compared to their male counterparts is inferior, but their placement among women puts them above average among women. In other words, the level of testosterone leads to a paradox: women are not permitted to have levels as high as men, but they are at an advantage compared to other women. Therefore, the first option involves putting the female hermaphrodite at a clear disadvantage compared to masculine colleagues and rivals. The second option implies harming the hopes of other female athletes who may have to compete against hermaphrodite athletes because the former would be at an obvious disadvantage. Even if this is a tragic dilemma, the point this case makes is that female hermaphrodite athletes are not in a situation as a result of their own decisions, but rather because they have been born with these sexual characteristics by a random act of nature.

Another problem that cannot be left untreated when it comes to judging hermaphrodite participation in sport is the fact that this condition manifests itself with levels of testosterone superior to the levels of the rest of women, and that acts as an advantage in some sports, but there are certain symptoms linked to hermaphroditism that can make success in other sports difficult. In effect, hermaphroditism tends to be linked to shorter stature, which mean that these individuals are (relatively) less apt for those sports where height is an advantage (basketball, volleyball, etc.). Another variant of hermaphroditism, known as Androgen Insensitivity Syndrome, causes the subject not to have any of the physical advantages linked to masculine sex, such as increased muscle mass. The problem with this phenotype causing this variation is that it is extremely variable and is difficult to predict (Schneider 2009). For those reasons, Wonkam, Fieggen, and Ramesar conclude:

> The number of genetic "abnormalities" concerning gender together with variable expression (Lee et al. 2006), and their complexity infers that the current IAAF gender policy is inadequate to cope with such cases. The IOC's revision of its stance on gender verification is long overdue. The policy needs to protect rights and privacy for athletes while safeguarding fairness of competition (Wonkam, Fieggen, and Ramesar 2010; 547).

Lastly, there is no direct link between any type of genetic anomaly and sport performance. An individual can be extraordinarily tall, but may not be flexible enough to play basketball well; another may have an above-average level of testosterone, but may not have the ability to make sacrifices required by elite sport or the intelligence necessary to plan strategies during a competition. That is, a genetic anomaly does not necessary manifest itself as necessarily providing a decisive advantage in sport. Successful performance in sport does not depend on just one factor but on an appropriate combination of a diverse set of physical and psychological characteristics.

If we add to these problems the fact that genetic tests have the potential to provoke psychological harm to women who are unaware of their suffering any type of sexual development disorder, the current policy of sport authorities on female hermaphrodite athletes must be thoroughly re-examined.

But the basic question in terms of sport has yet to be answered. This has its own rules, which have the objective—among others—of safeguarding the approximate equality of all the participants in a sporting event. Does the participation of a female hermaphrodite violate the core value of sport? No blanket answer can be given because the increase in physical performance generated by a higher level of testosterone is not always the same, and of course, this does not lead an individual to always win in competition. A simple example suffices to express my meaning: Semenya never overcame (or even got close) to Kratochvilova's times in the 800 metres. The South African athlete runs the 800 metres in 1 minute 55 seconds, while the Czechoslovakian holds the world record at

1 minute 53 seconds. Therefore, it would make more sense to consider the hormonal advantages of hermaphrodites as a random genetic factor.

However, the problem persists when the particular biological advantage goes beyond what is normal. Should measures prohibit that athlete from participating in competition against female athletes? An alternative in those cases would be to organize hermaphrodite competitions with that level of physical performance, but this does not seem viable due to the small number of those athletes. The solution may be to allow them to compete against men even though their chances of being successful are smaller. But this does not seem to be a fair solution either.

In my opinion, even when their advantages are extraordinary (something that is actually uncommon), hermaphrodites should be allowed to participate in female competitions. First of all, as I pointed out above, sport performance does not depend on one sole physiological factor. Secondly, neither is it out of the ordinary that certain individuals with outstanding physiological advantages participate. At the end of the day, athletes in basketball over 2.2 metres (7 feet) tall also have a remarkable advantage over the rest of the players. Or in swimming, an individual whose foot size is above average also has an advantage over other swimmers (Ian Thorpe wore a 52 in European sizes, 17 in the United States) and no thought has ever been giving to prohibiting them from participating.

Transexuals

Transexuals find themselves in a similar situation. These are individuals whose sexual identity is in conflict with their sexual anatomy. That is, a certain degree of disconformity is produced between their biological sex and their psychological sex. Like hermaphrodites, their situation does not correspond to a free decision but is rather the result of biological luck.

Nevertheless, the question concerning gender is further complicated due to cases of transexualism generated by anabolic steroid consumption. This is the case of the now man Andreas Krieger. Andreas in reality was born as a woman with the name Heidi. During childhood and adolescence she gained notoriety as a shot putter for the German Democratic Republic (GDR). She competed as a woman for East Germany in several international competitions, even winning the gold medal in the 1986 European Championship in Athletics. Unfortunately, as was the case with many GDR athletes at the time, she received large doses of anabolic steroids.

Heidi Krieger retired from track and field in 1990, and in 1997, accepting that steroids had left her with masculine features except for a masculine genital organ, she decided to undergo treatment that included sex reassignment surgery in order to become a man. After that time, she chased her name to Andreas. Krieger is now married to a former swimmer from East Germany, Ute Krause, who was also a victim of doping instigated by coaches. As a result of systematic doping that he suffered over those years, Krieger now suffers notable health problems that keep him from sleeping normally and from carrying out tasks that require great physical effort.

In 2000, Krieger testified in a lawsuit against Manfred Ewald, leader of the East German sports program and president of the GDR Olympic committee, and against Manfred Hoeppner, medical doctor. He testified that the medicine that they had given him during his time as a thrower had contributed to his transexuality. Both Ewald and Hoeppner were declared guilty as accomplices to the intentional bodily damage that they caused on athletes to whom anabolic steroids were given, even when they were underage. Given the repercussions in the Krieger case, an award is now given to those who stand out in the fight against doping. This prize is known as the Heidi Krieger Medal.

The Krieger case also brings about more questions. It must be asked if she was a woman with innate masculine traits or were they physiological traits that developed from the use of steroids. Said another way, was her masculinity natural (as is the case of Semenya) or artificial? If it is artificial, should there be any moral distinction? The Krieger case is distinct given that the consumption of steroids ended up leading to a physiological transformation that was encouraged by the sport authorities, and it was not an autonomous or desired decision.

But if an athlete did decide to consume anabolic steroids to improve his or her sport performance, and thus compete as a man assuming that the changes in his sexual identity are produced, would there be any moral objection? If the individual's decision is freely made and no others are harmed (something that would happen if allowed to compete in female competitions), where would the moral objection be? Evidently, voices would be heard pointing out that these are "unnatural" transformations, or as Michael Sandel says, contrary to what was "given and received," but the burden of proof would be on their side: What "nature" are they referring to? On the other hand, should this supposed "nature" take precedence over personal autonomy? Is it justifiable to prohibit those changes and stop them from pursuing plans of life that do not harm anyone, beyond offending another's "moral sensibility"? Fortunately, transsexual athletes were allowed to compete (under the condition that their sexual status was legally recognized and their hormonal operation had taken place two years prior to the competition) in the 2004 Athens Olympics. As was the case with hermaphrodite athletes, the decision regarding their participation in masculine or feminine competitions should not take into account their sexual identity.

CONCLUSIONS

My purpose in this chapter has been to analyse the main arguments that work against the traditional, but unjustified, discrimination against women in sport. After giving a brief history of the social foundation of this discrimination, I have examined three normative proposals that aim to establish conditions of equality among men and women in sport. These three conceptions are, firstly, the one that proposes established segregated sports for men and women; secondly, that of extreme equalization; and thirdly, that of gender equity. After laying out the pros and cons of each one, I believe it is more reasonable and feasible to accept the last proposal with a few caveats.

The second major section of this chapter has been devoted to examining two cases in which the sex of the athletes is in doubt: transsexuals and hermaphrodites. In both cases, I have tried to demonstrate that the restrictive regulation in both groups is unjustified and, therefore, recognition of their equal right to participate in female competitions should be accorded, save the (very infrequent) cases where their physiology leads them to have a substantial advantage over their rivals.

FOUR

Sport, War, and Violence

The dark side of sport can be seen in that it is constantly used to highlight three aspects of doubtful morality. Firstly, I highlight the analogy drawn been sport and war. Secondly, I point to the critique that sport involves and generates violence between participants. In this section I have focused part of my analysis specifically on boxing, given its leading spot in terms of violence in sport. Thirdly, sport has been criticized, as regards the admiration lauded upon winning athletes, for promoting emotions and beliefs among fans similar to those produced by fascism.

SPORT AND WAR

Sport has been deemed a subliminal, ritualistic war exercise. To use the words of Robert Simon, the discipline of sport can be characterized as "miniaturized version[s] of war" (Simon 1991; 64) due to the underlying or explicit confrontation between individuals or teams, as well as to the use of strategies, tactics and—on occasion—violence. There are three areas where analogies can be drawn between sport and war: 1) the face-off between two opposing sides; 2) the use of strategies; and 3) tolerance of the use of violence to ensure victory (at least in some disciplines). I will concentrate on points 1 and 3, that is, on conflict and violence as elements linking sport with war.

One of the principle grounds for comparing sport and war is the confrontation between players and teams to obtain a common, but exclusive, goal: victory. As is the usual case in war, the primary sport confrontation is a zero sum game; one contender wins all, while the other loses all. Even though it is true that both parties have an interest in starting the "game," indicating a certain element of collaboration between contenders, at the core there is also a desire to defeat the opponent and be victorious in the encounter.

In terms of violence, it is may be cliché but still true, that competitive sport reflects and fosters behaviors and attitudes that are innate to war. In sport (at least in some important disciplines) and war, violence is involved. In effect, in some sports, and not exactly the least popular, violence is not permitted unless it is a tool to reach the desired goal: victory. In some disciplines violence is obviously present, as in boxing (and other types of fighting), where competitions have even ended in death as a consequence of the exchange of pugilistic blows. Unfortunately, other sports also contain violent actions that cause severe harm to the health of athletes and have also caused death. This has been the case in soccer, rugby, fencing, hockey, etc. While I will return to this point later on, the matter at hand causing concern in society in general is the extent to which violence should be permitted in sport. Should the fact that violent action takes place within a framework of mutual consent of the participants exclude the imposition of civil and criminal law sanctions for similar actions performed outside the sport arena? While sport is not the only area where violent activity takes place, it is likely the leading social environment where violence is not only tolerated, it is actually praised as an important part of society.

Given the relevance of these factors (conflict, strategy, and violence) in sport, as well as the imitation of war, it is not surprising to note that the sport pages are full of bellicose metaphors: "conquer," "battle," "death," "destruction," "victory," "honor," and "prestige" to name a few. Athletes as well as journalists and fans experience extreme emotions through the use of violent and warlike expressions.

It would not make much sense, however, to take the analogy between war and sport too far, as the generally negative rejection produced by war versus the generally positive enthusiasm generated by sport in current society would not be easily understood. The differences between both phenomena seem to be more relevant than their similarities. Thus, it seems obvious that the sense and restrictions in the use of violence are different in both arenas, apart from the fact that it is a permitted means in both systems. Victory in war is sought "at all costs," which can involve a sacrifice of goods, but sport injury would not be permitted (to a certain extent) because athletes do not want to lose at any cost. While in war, one's life and physical integrity are at peril, and one's life is subordinate to obtaining victory, in sport there are normative and institutional barriers whose goal is to safeguard the life and health of the athletes. That is, violence and its related effects are relatively permitted in sport, but they are subordinated to the preservation of life and health as morally superior values.

Connected to this investment in the main values in war and sport, something similar also occurs with the concern and interest in victory.

The sense of victory is completely different in each environment. In both cases, physical effort has victory over the rival as a final goal, but the meaning of the victory is distinct. In competitive sport, athletes seek "honor in success," and from that they value the game as victorious, but also the display of a certain excellence in techniques used to obtain that victory. Related to the importance of displaying skills, abilities and techniques in sport, victory here is, unlike what happens in war; here it is normally evaluated by judges or referees of the competition, with standards respected by all. What's more, technical or aesthetic efforts also influence the final result. On the other hand, in bellicose conflict, victory is sought as an end in and of itself; even though it is not ideal, an individual may be willing to lose the most precious and dearest goods to the combatants. And even though there are rules as to how conflict should develop (the concept known as "ius in bello," law in war), it is als: true that the judgment mechanisms to enforce these rules and principles have been improving over the last century, but they are still very precarious.

Last, but not least, as Huizinga and Suits have highlighted, both phenomena respond to totally opposed human interests. Sport, in terms of the show of sport, has primarily achieved remarkable economic, social and political relevance in recent decades but is not considered "serious" activity, but rather an expression of recreational instinct. On the other hand, war is the maximum expression of "serious" activity with nearly absolute concern for victory to the subordination of goods most appreciated by human beings (life, health, security, and respect).

However, there are still sports that are excessively violent in and of themselves, ones that allow violent action to take place within the rules. There are not yet means established that are powerful enough to discourage the violent action that constitutes infractions of the norms.

SPORT AND VIOLENCE

As I have indicated above, violence forms part of the practice of sport, beyond the differences of the meaning and role that it plays in war. But before I analyze the role of violence in sport, I would like to make two caveats. The first is that my primary analysis is of elite professional sport, what some authors have called the sport-spectacle, and not educational and recreational sport. The second warning regards the type of violence dealt with in this section. In this sense, endogenic and exogenic violence can be distinguished, although both types can be linked in the sense that they feed into each other (Gamero 2006; 19). The former's place is at the core of sport itself, as foreseen and regulated by the codes that govern its practice (as is the case in the violence eventually exercised in the infraction of these rules). The second type, exogenic violence, is violence exercised by fans in relation to the sport. There is no doubt that currently this type of violence constitutes a social problem of utmost importance. Unfortunately, there have been many episodes of violence in recent years. Perhaps the most famous of these was the tragedy in the Heysel Stadium with the violent deaths of rival fans: on May 29, 1985, shortly before the start of the European Cup where Juventus of Turin played against Liverpool, twenty-nine supporters of the Italian team were killed and six hundred others injured as a result of an avalanche of Liverpool fans. In another incident, in 1998 Aitor Zabaleta, a Real Sociedad fan, was stabbed to death by an Atlético de Madrid fan. A similar incident took place when one Espanyol fan died at the hands of the "Boixos Nois," radical followers of Barcelona FC (Gómez 2007). Of course, when this type of violence in sport is talked about, one must be aware that 90 percent of it is concentrated in soccer. Beyond the social relevance and danger caused by this violence as well as the studies about its different causes, my field of attention is not on this area, but rather on the violence within the sporting discipline. The issue that I raise is to identify limits placed on endogenic violence, and to do that, it would be opportune to characterize and define it.

But the concept of violence does not appear to be easy to delineate; however, I will enumerate here several reasons for this difficulty (Parry 1998):

1. Different perspectives between distinct disciplines that have dealt with violence have not used uniform terminology since they observe the same phenomenon from distinctly different points of view (for example, sociology may pay attention to social factors of violence while psychology examines psychological aspects).
2. The error of observing and analyzing violence (and aggression) as unified concepts, as if all forms were aspects of the same phenomenon, or if all of the manifestations had the same cause.
3. This is a concept loaded with moral, social and political meaning (Smith 2003; 204) dependent on personal analysis within the context an invidivual is working; the characterization can take on a different form. As Smith points out, the observation of the same act, carried out by an individual under normal circumstances, can be characterized as violence, but the same act carried out by security forces under mandate by the State is called "force."
4. The difficulty in establishing distinctions regarding concepts that are somewhat related, like "aggression."

In any case, my objective in this section is to establish the distinction between violence and aggression. In this sense, there seems to exist a certain agreement between a minimal characterization of violence and of aggression, especially from a social sciences perspective, so that the notion of aggression is largely characterized as a concept beyond the scope of violence. Aggression includes conduct that aims to harm others, physically or psychologically. However, violence refers exclusively to the physical aspect of aggression, i.e., to the conduct that aims to or is carried out with the intent to physically harm another person (Dixon 2001; 20, Smith 2003; 200), whether this is with direct or indirect intent (the prediction that the produced action will inflict harm).

The fact is that violence in sport has never been viewed as true violence. Save some specific cases, the courts have been traditionally reticent to judge even the most scandalous incidents of bloodshed in sport. Experts in criminal law do not have a unified voice on the position of violence in sport. Even though they may have violated the rules, the majority of athletes who use violence as well as the victims view it as "part of the game." As Ríos points out,

> There is some independence of the sport field since this activity has its own legal instruments, its own institutions and authorities and it has turned into a "island" located to some distance of the rest of mechanisms of social control, amongst other, of the Penal Law (Ríos 2010; 618).

In spite of the fact that public opinion about violence in sport has been changing over the last few decades, fans often applaud players who act violently, whereas in other situations their reaction would have been the opposite, or they may have even considered the action criminal (Schneider quotes Gary Bettman, commissioner of the National Hockey League, showing that he is aware that followers of this sport consider fights between players to be an intrinsic part of hockey and given that many followers anticipate and enjoy violence in the game, leaders of this sport are inclined to continue allowing fights as "part of the game" [Schneider 2009; 180]). However, this panorama is starting to change. The role of violence in sport is an issue that began to be questioned a few decades ago, and in this sense, some authors claim that these actions cannot be exempt from the Law, whether this be civil or criminal variety.

The first legal ruling in favor of submitting violent actions that occurred as part of sport competition to the same rules as any other violent act probably dates back to the late nineteenth century:

> No rules or practice of any game whatever can make that lawful which is unlawful by the law of the land; and the law of the land says you shall not do that which is likely to cause the death of another. For instance, no persons can by agreement go out to fight with deadly weapons, doing by agreement what the law says shall not be done, and thus shelter themselves from the consequences of their acts. Therefore, in one way you need not concern yourself with the rules of football (Hechter 1977; 444, quoted by Smith 2003; 204).

These words were pronounced by Lord Justice Bramwell as instructions to the jury in the 1878 *Regina v. Bradshaw* case, in which a soccer player was accused of homicide after a game where a player was injured during the game played under association rules, and then died afterwards. The accused was acquitted, but the judge's ruling has been cited in the United States by those who want sport not to be excluded from the laws that regulate our behavior.

Several years later, in 1895 in Syracuse, New York, Robert Fitzsimmons organized a public boxing exhibition, sparring with Riordan. As a result of the fight, Riordon was knocked out from repeated blows to the head and he died five hours later. Fitzsimmons was accused of homicide. The judge directed the jury as follows:

> If the rules of the game and the practices of the game are reasonable, are consented to by all engaged, are not likely to induce serious injury, or to end life, if then, as a result of the game, an accident happens, it is excusable homicide (Hechter 1977; 443, quoted by Smith 2003; 204).

Similar to what happened in the *Regina* case, he was acquitted. What is most valuable and noteworthy in this case is that the rules and practice of the game were taken into consideration to determine eventual criminal liability, a precedent contrary to that which had been established in the *Regina v. Bradshaw* case. Nevertheless, judges in the United States and in the other countries are still reluctant to return guilty verdicts under criminal law for injuries produced in sport competitions.

To more thoroughly examine this issue regarding the scope of violence that should be permitted in sport, and subsequently determine to what extent the justice system and criminal law should intervene in sport, several distinctions should also be made. In the first place, the types of sport and the type of violence should be different in each case. Bakker (quoted by Gamero 2006; 43) distinguishes between combat and contact sport, and sport where this violence is not necessary. The first two types are those that need to be regulated in terms of violence. At that same time, it is necessary to more accurately define the scope of the violence problem within these sport because it seems clear that cases of violence in sport that do not generate severe injuries do not raise any special moral or legal difficulties as these are admitted and accepted as a natural result of the practice of sport itself. The problem with violence in sport arises when an athlete is severely injured. It is here where dissenting voices can be heard regarding the eventual tolerance or prohibition of such violence. Authors who advocate for prohibition highlight that the perpetrators of these violent acts (under certain requirements) should be judged under the Penal Code or the crime of assault, which establishes that the assault was intentional and required medical attention and treatment (Article 147 of the Spanish Penal Code). Said another way, the minor damage to health, which an athlete receives due to a violent act during a sport competition, that does not require assistance and medical treatment will not be the subject of evaluation by referees on the field, by courts or by disciplinary sport committees. The problem arises when severe injuries result from the violent acts; to what extent should they be tolerated in sport and, is it appropriate that they be judged in ordinary courts?

Injuries by Actions Permitted by the Rules

This category of violence in sport comprises all significant physical contact carried out within the rules of a discipline: holds, blocks, collisions, jabs and blows of any other type. Such contact is inherent to sports such as boxing, wrestling, ice hockey, rugby and—to a lesser extent—soccer, basketball, water polo, handball, etc. It is taken for granted that when individuals choose to participate in any of those sports, they automatically accept that those contacts (holds, blows, collisions, jabs and blows according to the case at hand) will be inevitable, and that there is a certain likelihood of mild to severe physical harm.

In legal terms, it is accepted that players consent to receive these actions and possible injury (volenti non fit injuria). Suppose, in a rugby game, a player powerfully tackles a rival but does so within the scope of blocking rules. As a result of the attack, the player is severely injured. Or in the case of boxing, imagine one of the pugilists violently hits his rival's face in such a way that the opponent's nose is fractured. These situations are perfectly possible, but they would carry no sanctions given that they were carried out within the scope of the rules.

Even though this is the case, if the victim athlete decided to file a suit in civil court, the possibility of receiving compensation for damages would be null. Technically, the law establishes that if the defender who performed the block could have predicted that the act would severely injure his opponent, that there was (a certain degree of) premeditation in injuring the opponent, then he is guilty. However, given that the injury took place in a sport context, the legal solution is different given that any blow received within the rules of a sport is legally allowed under the law (Smith 2003; 205).

Nonetheless, when physical contact becomes disproportionate, in order to obtain a means allowed by the rules of the game, then these actions reach a new level, that of brutality. In these cases, the athlete inflicts harm on a rival which is done as part of a strategy. But when there has been certain abuse or disproportionate use of force, if the act is recognized within the rules of the game, the corresponding sanction is given out on the playing field itself by the referee.

Cases of brutality in sport have always existed. Smith recounts the tragic situation of American football towards the close of the nineteenth century when teams played more aggressively than was reasonable. For example, a newspaper of the time reported that during a 1893 Harvard-Yale game, seven players left the field in sad shape, with broken legs, back bones destroyed and one had even lost an eye (Smith 2003; 206).

Along the same lines, another report highlighted that in the 1905 season eighteen players had died and 159 had been severely injured. The scandal and level of concern about this sport reached such a level that President Roosevelt convened representatives from the leading teams to demand that the level of brutality decrease. American football has become considerably more civilized since then, especially due to sophisticated protective gear worn by players on the field. Nevertheless, it still continues to be a "harsh" sport in which brutality forms a part of the "rules of the game," as statistics from the 1980s show: nearly 318,000 players in each season had to receive medical treatment as a result of injuries received on the field.

Injury by Actions Permitted According to the "Ethos" of the Sport

In this category, violent action that may actually be prohibited by the rules of the sport, habitually forms part of competition and is accepted by referees, players and fans alike. They are acts tolerated by the "ethos" of the sport. An example from football happens when defense jostles with offense during a corner kick in order to be in a better position to defend against a throw-in. There is also the case of playing with arms spread wide (or hitting the ball with an elbow) against a rival in order to block a rival who is trying to get possession from the back. On several occasions, these moves result in severe blows to the opponent's face, but they tend to be categorized as accidents of the game. Such action is not permitted by the rules but tends to be tolerated by the "ethos" of the sport.

These cases of aggression brush the limit of prohibited violence that usually has to be decided by referees or judges on the field of play, although sometimes the cases are appealed to higher-level sport authorities. However, in general, sanctions imposed almost never result in any type of sanction beyond a suspension from a future match, or occasionally a fine.

The explanation for the fact that these violent actions are not judged by ordinary courts is that they are generally tolerated and accepted by most of the parties involved in the game. They would form part of the "ethos of the game" that grants permission to take part in the outcome of the game. As E. Gamero highlights, "traditionally, athletes have been very permissive in this area; they do not tend to intervene in squabbles amongst themselves, and they accept injuries as moves of the game or as moments of passing disturbance which should be forgiven without punishment" (Gamero 2006; 20). The problem arises when there are doubts as to whether the violent act falls within the so-called ethos of the game. These are cases when the aggressor used excessive or improper lex artis (law of the skill) or had the sole intention of causing harm to the opponent. There may be clear cases where circumstances could be proven but, instead, fall in the shadows. The most notorious and hotly debated case in Spanish sport happened in a football match between Seville and Mallorca in which a Mallorca player was bashed by a Seville player's elbow, causing a heart attack and admittance to the ICU. According to the aggressor's description, his actions would normally fall under what is called "protecting the ball," but other players contend that he had purposely left the ball in order to intentionally assault the other player. Some consider this as a "move of the game," while others claim that the Seville player's action went beyond the limits that the rules and "ethos" of the game establish, and for that reason, they would become susceptible to criminal action (Ríos 2010; 635) since Penal Code requirements for assault are present: intentional assault that requires medical assistance and treatment (Spanish Penal Code article 145). Recently the Argentinian soccer player Camoranesi (who has now been nationalized as an Italian citizen) has been condemned for an injury committed in 1994 against Pizzo, a player of the rival team. According to the Supreme Court of Justice of Buenos Aires (Argentina) he will have to pay 32,000 euros plus interest in damages for the aggression that was realized during a match in 1994. In its ruling, the courts commented, "Although Camoranesi's action cannot be described as intentional, it indicates a notorious clumsiness, an excess in the practice of the sport, which is abnormal and avoidable and contrary to the rules of the sport." Meanwhile, the doctors found that Pizzo's knee injury, which required several surgical interventions, reduced his mobility to 39 percent.

Another distinct issue is whether sport authorities should tolerate as fact that an "ethos" of violence has developed in a sport discipline. In cases where the level of violence has reached such a point where it would be justified to modify the rules so that these violent acts are not permitted, and that carrying them out would lead to some sort of punitive action. This is precisely what President Roosevelt intended when he met with the leaders of American football teams and asked them to reduce the level of violence, as I mentioned above.

Injuries from Actions Beyond the Scope of "Moves of the Game"

Actions that are outside the scope of "moves of the game" are carried out in a competition and not only violate the formal rules, they also blatantly infringe on the use of sport and produce severe harm to a rival. These actions normally take place during the game, but are, at the time they are carried out, foreign to the "scope of the game." It is this type of action that has caught the attention of jurists who question if it is appropriate to apply the penal law in these cases. Think of a violent act resulting in a somewhat severe injury to a rival, an act that was produced during a game, but outside the scope of the game. For example, two players are exchanging blows on the field of play, but they are 50 metres away from the action with the ball on the field. This case arrived at the courts (Decision of Balearic Islands Court on June 29, 2001), and a ruling of criminal assault was handed down. Another case arising from a football game also made it to the courts due to the injuries produced by a foul from behind "without the intention or the chance of getting possession of the ball." Another much more famous case that never made it to criminal court, but which has similar characteristics, is Mike Tyson's bite that took off part of Evander Holyfield's ear during a boxing match. And to round things out, other more recent cases that may fit in this category are the famous assault where the Real Madrid coach, J. Mourinho, stuck a finger in the eye of the FC Barcelona assistant coach, "Tito" Vilanova, as well as in another Real Madrid vs. FC Barcelona match where a spectator was injured in the face as a result of Messi's shot toward the stands that took place while the clock was stopped. Let us imagine that in one of these cases the victim had been severely injured. Could they have brought criminal charges against their assailants?

Injuries Produced by Reckless or Excessively Violent Acts

These two criteria are commonly used in ruling on the justification or illegality of a violent act with harmful results from a sporting competition. In spite of the fact that they present obvious problems resulting from vaguely defined criteria, it is certain there are clear cases where it can be concluded that a player has been violent and has used an excessive degree of violence to gain an advantage over a rival. In this way, a football defender tries to steal the ball from a forward by throwing himself or herself at the forward, instead of keeping his/her feet firmly planted on the ground, and the defender hits the rival in the knees. Another example may be the blow at the end of the last World Cup final match that the Spanish player Xabi Alonso received from the Dutch player who kicked Xabi in the chest with three spikes and may have broken his bone. These cases give rise to serious doubts given that, on the one hand they meet all the necessary requirements for criminal assault, but on the other hand the "ethos" of the sport deems that in spite of the injuries received, they should be dealt with by disciplinary committees or sport courts.

In in contrast, in the United States there is a growing tendency for victims of violent acts to file suit in criminal court. In effect, it has stopped being an exception that victims of sport injuries received during competition take legal action. But the number of suits filed compared to the number of injuries produced as a result of these violent acts is still low. There are several reasons that lead athletes to not take legal action against the aggressors; some cite the "ethos" that the players themselves have, while others have legal reasons. Among those who refer to "ethos" as the underlying reason is an unwritten conviction that disputes between athletes must be resolved on the field and forgotten once the game is over. Those who do not follow this rule may be looked down upon by the rest of their teammates for breaking the rules of "fair play" (Gamero 2006; 58). In addition, an athlete who is the victim today may be the aggressor tomorrow, and with this foresight the athlete does not want it to become common practice to take legal action of this type. Linked to this way of thinking, it has been pointed out that injuries produced on the playing field are seen as less severe by athletes and society in general (Ríos 2010; 607).

Among the legal reasons that are alleged in favor of criminal impunity to sporting injuries derived from violent acts, they highlight:

1. The fact that there has been previous consent to participate in a sporting competition.
2. The theory of the chance case according to which there is no premeditation in producing these injuries.

By following the line of reasoning in the first argument, it has been pointed out that athletes accept risks that naturally arise from the sport that they freely choose to play. That is, they freely choose to put their health at risk. This argument has found support in several legal rulings where the courts have been reticent to punish violent injuries based on the fact that consent operates to the exclusion of liability (Navas 2006; 334).

The theory of chance case relies on the conviction that athletes do not participate with fraudulent intentions, but rather, they carry out the practice of sport with recreational or leisure goals and not to harm others. For this reason, it is understood that injuries that may result are chance cases and lack premeditation (Navas 2006; 333).

However, there is an increasingly strong tendency among jurists who claim that these actions can be dealt with under the scope of criminal law. Regarding the sport "ethos" argument, according to which violent injuries should be substantiated within the sport environment, the objection has been raised that social perception about a fact is not always stable, but changes with the passing of time. In addition, such a perception can be guided by irrational considerations; it can be influenced by prejudice, persistent patterns of thought, attachment to tradition, etc., in such a way that there is no value in this justification. What is relevant about a collective perception or opinion regarding a topic of social importance is not whether there is less or more social support, but rather if that social belief is morally justified.

Regarding the theory of consent, the value of tacit consent granted by athletes when they concede to play has been questioned. From this critical standpoint, consent is limited to assuming risks derived from actions or bodily contact permitted by the rules of the game and by the use of those rules, but consent is not given for suffering injury resulting from violent bodily contact that is prohibited by the rules of the game or the uses of the sport (Smith 2003; 207). If it is accepted that health is an unavailable good, then there is no consent that justifies the causation of injuries. For this reason, it is considered under the criminal code that consent of the injured individual does not exclude the criminal liability of the perpetrator, although it does act to attenuate it.

Lastly, the thesis that athletes act in good faith only counts as a defeasible assumption. If it is proven that during the course of the game the aggressor had the intent to harm another, even if he/she acted recklessly or if the injury took place far removed from the scope of the game, then the assumption lacks justification and will be defeated. That is, the act could be considered as grounds for possible criminal punishment for the aggressor.

Thus, there must be a distinction drawn between three possible cases for violence in sport, from lesser to greater severity. In the first case, injuries produced by violent acts that are permitted by the rules of the game should continue to fall under the scope of the arbiter or judge of the sport competition itself. Currently, these types of acts are not sanctioned. In the second case, injuries produced within the scope of "sport ethos" offer a higher degree of indeterminacy, but it seems justified to think that such actions should continue to be the realm of the judges of the sport themselves or the sport courts. In the third case, injuries produced by violent actions removed from the "scope of the game," or which involve excessive or reckless use of violence, should be considered under the jurisdiction of the courts of record given that they can appeal neither to the protection of the rules nor to the "ethos" of the sport. Lastly, these excessive or reckless, violent acts that result in severe injuries are difficult to categorize as strictly falling under wrongdoing in sport or criminal wrongdoing. Possibly, the solution of each specific case would need to be judged on the particular circumstances of individual cases.

THE CASE OF BOXING

Boxing continues to be one sport that has generated the most discussion due to the role that violence plays in it and the enormous physical consequences of that violence. Simon (1993) points out that more than 350 boxers have died in the United States in fights taking place since 1945, a figure which does not take into account the numerous injuries, especially to the brain, that many boxers have suffered.

Independently from the conceptual problems surrounding the term "violence," which are significant in limiting the phenomenon and its eventual justification (Parry 1998), two main arguments have been directed against this sport. Firstly, critics claim that the practice itself damages the boxer himself, and based on paternalistic justification, it should be prohibited. Additionally, it has been alleged that boxing damages society, specifically the shared morality of members of a society. The problem with the first objection is that prohibiting boxing would affect the autonomous decision-making ability of individuals who wish to participate in this activity, and it is difficult to maintain that such individuals are basically incompetent, i.e., they lack the ability to reason and thus cannot decide on their own life plans, even when it is the case that boxing produces severe physical harm that could even involve death.

The second objection is even more fragile. Nevertheless, Dixon has attempted to get beyond this objection by pointing out that boxing may be immoral given that it is offensive to the majority morals of the society (Dixon 2001; 398). As it is well known, this argument has been Lord Devlin's point of support in his debate in the mid-twentieth century with Herbert Hart on considering homosexuality a crime in England. Dixon updates Devlin's ideas to claim that given that the boxer means to intentionally hit his opponent and cause the greatest possible amount of damage in order to win the fight, such actions should be considered immoral in that they lead the opponent to be treated like a mere object. This action does not only concern the boxer himself; it also involves spectators and society as a whole who would obtain pleasure from the misfortune of the loser. In short, according to Dixon, these actions would not only be immoral, they would border on being sadistic. From another point of view, such an objection would arise from moral perfectionism, if it were the case that the immoral character of boxing did have roots so much in the beliefs and attitudes of the majority of a society, and in a certain ideal of the good life that the State tries to bolster in society, without concern for if it were really accepted by the citizens. Said another way, obtaining pleasure from the suffering of another person and enjoying the public display of violence and its harmful consequences on the physical well-being of the other individual would not be a "good life plan" that a well-ordered society should tolerate, or much less promote.

A compromise solution, with which I basically agree, is offered by Simon (1991). He does not find moral reasons to prohibit boxing since that would involve unjustified paternalism of the law. However, given its negative characteristics in terms of the moral perspective, it would be feasible to modify the rules to avoid greater harmful consequences to boxers' health from taking place. This is what happened with fencing, which was the object of a past rule revision in order to lessen the number of injuries and the risk to life. It would be reasonable to carry out similar reforms in boxing in order to reduce the danger it entails to the boxers by introducing another type of protective head gear. In this way, what is truly relevant about boxing would not be inflicting the greatest amount of harm on the rival but rather the expression of technical skills of the boxers. Additionally, with this solution the State would not act as the paternalistic agent prohibiting boxing, but would not "get its hands dirty" by promoting it either. Rather, it would allow the success of boxing to remain in the hands of those interested in maintaining the practice of the sport (Schneider 2009). It goes without saying that this tolerance is only permissible as it relates to adult individuals who are in full command of their faculties to guide their own lives, but it does not apply to minors, whose participation in fights, even training fights, the State would be justified in prohibiting.

SPORT AND FASCISTOID ADMIRATION

Another negative angle of sport has been explored by Swedish philosopher Torbjörn Tännsjö (1998), for whom one of the essential factors of contemporary sport is the admiration that athletes arouse among fans, but under this layer of care, deference and adulation, there is a hidden psychological trait that pertains to fascism itself. In effect, it is well known that the winners of elite sport competition, especially the more popular sport, are elevated to the peak of fame and glorification. They become idols for a society and normally become role models, especially for youth. But

> our admirations for the achievement of the great sports heroes, such as the athletes that triumph at the Olympics, reflects a fascistoid ideology. While nationalism may be dangerous and has often been associated with fascism, what is going on in our enthusiasm for individual athletic heroes is even worse. Our enthusiasm springs from the very core of fascist ideology (Tännsjö 1998; 430).

What Tännsjö attempts to show is that fans of elite sport who follow athletes' attainments and achievements tend to generate dangerous emotions. Firstly, they provoke and foster nationalistic emotions in spectators. This nationalistic feeling can lead to undesirable results such as individual subordination to the collective interest of the nation. Secondly, admiration for the winners of different sport practices, especially those with great popular following, constitutes an expression of disdain for weakness that was characteristic of Nazism.

This is what Tännsjö views as the principle problem in sport, not so much the link with nationalism:

> My thesis is this: When we give up nationalism as a source of our interest in elite sports activities, when we give up our view of individual sportsmen and teams as representatives or "our" nation, when we base our interest in sports on a more direct fascination for the individual winners of these events—we move from something that is only contingently associated with nazism (nationalism) to something that is really at the core of nazism (a contempt for weakness) (Tännsjö 1998; 432).

To support this thesis, he highlights that admiration for winners goes hand in hand with assessing athlete's skill as excellent, which make them valuable. This excellence mainly springs from the strength they display in the sporting competition. At the same time, Tännsjö's opinion is that there is an indivisible relationship between admiration for the winner and disdain for the loser:

> So if we see a person as specially valuable because of his excellences, and if the excellences is an manifestation of strength (in a very literal sense), then this must mean that other people, who do not win the fair competition, those who are comparatively weak, are less valuable. The most natural feeling associated with these value judgments is con tempt. It is expressed in the popular saying: "being second is being the first of one among the losers" (Tännsjö 1998; 433).

Tännsjö tries to support his thesis about the shared emotions felt by sport fans by highlighting that the main competitions that generate a greater degree of public interest are those that have absolute elite participation. The admiration and interest of the fan is principally, and almost exclusively, directed at those athletes who are at the top of the game, a manifestation of their high degree of excellence. In contrast, interest falls off sharply when the participants in competitions (whether it is individual or team) are women or disabled athletes, given that in both cases the degree of sporting excellence tends to be lower than that of men, as Tännsjö points out:

> In any case, if we are forced to choose, what we, the vast majority of us, want most to watch are competitions involving the absolute elite, not the Olympics for handicapped people (Tännsjö 1998; 436).

However, Tännsjö's conception has been questioned by Tamburrini, who has raised several objections.

Admiration for winners can result from reasons other than fascination with "power," and in any case, the lack of interest in losers does not necessarily lead to being equated with disdain for them. There is no contradiction for admiring the winner and lack of disdainful attitudes for the loser. In other words, those who come in second may not deserve our attention (Tamburrini 2000; 116).

In effect, Tamburrini rightly points out that, in general, admiration for winning athletes does not only depend on strength, but on a broader set of excellent qualities. If this were the case, admiration for them would not only be fascistoid, it would also be chauvinistic. In reality, Tamburrini highlights that the object of admiration is not only athletes' strength "but rather their cultural expressions of excellence" (Tamburrini 2000; 114), which may be the expression of a varied set of qualities. In this sense, Tamburrini gives several examples, like gymnastics, in which women are more greatly appreciated than men, given that they express different talents and sometimes considerably better ones. Think about the admiration that Nadia Comaneci commanded at her time, something that has not been exceeded or even equaled by any male gymnast. Something similar is seen in tennis, where the greater strength of men is ruining the sport by making rallies and volleys more infrequent. In contrast, it is easier to see "good tennis" between women and in this way enjoy the more appreciated qualities of this sport: placing the ball, rallies, a variety of swings, etc.

But this objection can also be raised by the differing manifestations of skill within a single sport. In this way, for example, a footballer is sometimes admired for "powerful qualities," like strength, aggression, endurance and a desire to make a comeback. But in other contexts, fans appreciate technical skills like ball handling, an appreciation for the game, elegance in dribbling, etc.

In addition, Tamburrini highlights that the athletes who place second in sport competition may have been outstanding in some particular quality, even being better than the victor. Besides, there may be the case where "both the winner and the second-best might' have broken the world record for the sport in question. The fact that the next-best can also demonstrate this level of partial excellence can, in my opinion, neutralize the implicit disdain" (Tamburrini 2000; 117).

Elite sport may provide role models that, instead of fostering fascistoid sentiments, can generate attitudes that negate racism and discrimination against ethnic minorities.

Following the supposition that there is a necessary relationship between a successful sport achievement and admiration for an athlete as characterized by Tännsjö, it would then be necessary to highlight, as Tamburrini points out, that triumphant athletes belong to ethnic minorities and could have a positive effect on this group.

In effect, the progressive democratization of the world in the course of recent decades has allowed athletes and sportspeople in many sporting disciplines who are ethnic minorities to obtain victories and set records. This has led to them being the object of admiration not only by spectators who belong to the same racial, ethnic or religious group, but also by fans from other countries with different racial, ethnic and religious communities. This allows Tamburrini to make the conclusion:

> This appears to me to be of the utmost relevance in the current political situation where racist and neo-nazi trends threaten to distort the values inculcated in society. Any serious discussion on the moral status of elite sports must pay attention to this matter (Tamburrini 2000; 118).

In sum, I think that just as Tamburrini has shown, Tännsjö's assertion regarding the fascistoid nature of admiration for winning athletes is exaggerated. However, there is another aspect of the admiration of athletes that has been increasing with the passage of time and is deserving of criticism. Athletes, especially in those more popular disciplines, have not only become idols, but also life role models for many spectators, especially for children and adolescents (but also for parents). On many occasions, such admiration hides other factors that are present in success in sport which may not be so valuable. Firstly, there are many young athletes who do not become idols. After their athletic career—which takes place in the years where they would be trained for a work life—is finished, they lack an alternative life plan. Secondly, even in cases where young athletes triumph, they may be incapable of handling their success. In effect, given that many young people have lived in an environment of praise and richness, after their sport career is over, it becomes hard to live a normal life. There are enough known cases of athletes who become depressed, who have resorted to drugs or who have even committed suicide. The problem then is not only for them, but also for those to whom they have been a source of inspiration and those who have focused their life plan on sport. In this sense, the critique regarding the placement of sport idols on a pedestal is not because they generate fascist attitudes, but rather their deficient life plans.

CONCLUSIONS

In this chapter it has been my aim to analyze three critiques that have historically been directed at sport: 1) its link with war; 2) its use of violence; and 3) its disdain for losers. After briefly summarizing the main arguments that these critiques are based on, I have attempted to dismantle these main theses and save sport from contaminants. Regarding the analogy with war, I have claimed that in spite of having some factors in common with war, the sense of victory and violence that appear in some sport disciplines is very different from what is found in war. In addition, in no case in sport does the pursuit of victory intentionally put athletes' life at risk.

As regards the use of violence in some sport disciplines, the strategy that I have followed is to clarify the meaning of violence and to later examine how violence in most disciplines is contained by the rules and institutions that establish the legitimate frameworks for its use, and in so doing, they discourage the excessive and reckless expression of violence.

Lastly, following the arguments of the Swedish philosopher Tännsjö, I have summarized his critique that states that in sports' glorification of only the winners, disdain for the losers is implied and, in this sense, there is a strong connection with fascist ideology. Tamburrini, among others, has tried to dismantle this argumentative framework by highlighting that there is no logical connection between admiring the winner and disdaining the loser, given that there are cases in which the second best in a competition is also the object of praise. In addition, the Argentine author correctly highlighted that the victories obtained by ethnic and disadvantaged minorities may generate attitudes that are contrary to racism and discrimination against those minorities. Lastly, I have pointed out that admiration for athletes can be criticized for reasons other than its supposed fascist nature: the most elite popular sport put idols on pedestals who, in many cases, generate deficient life plan models.

FIVE

Sport, Politics, and Nationalism

Soccer is the more modern religion that has arrived to Europe.
—Manuel Vázquez Montalbán, Spanish writer

Sport is manifested in a variety of different ways, making it difficult to reduce the phenomenon of sports to the lowest common denominator. Historically, sporting competition, whether individual or team-based, has had the central goal of either reaching the highest possible standard of excellence in a concrete discipline or of hierarchically ranking athletes, according to the results attained, or to the display of different abilities.

Another defining characteristic of sport has been that it has been thought of as an activity not contaminated by politics. Sport, as it was conceived of by Baron de Coubertin, ought to be neutral with regard to political ideology and should remain isolated from political pressures from the State. According to Coubertin, beyond the level internal to a society, international sport should appear to be a neutral spiritual figure that possesses the necessary prestige in the face of the people of the world to treat all the results equally, i.e., without taking into account nations, political systems or group ownership (Brohm 1982; 201).

This vision of sport corresponds to the apoliticization of sport, a theoretical concept that maintains the absolute independence of the practice of sport from politics and which possibly has been, and continues to be, the dominant position among sport theorists, operators, and sport authorities at the domestic and international levels (Aguilera 1992; 13). It suffices to remember, for example, that the members of the IOC do not act as representatives of their nations of origin in order that they might avoid political influences.

Nevertheless, objections have been raised to this point of view. Firstly, it seems obvious that such a claim, if it has any meaning and is true regarding elite or professional sport, it is by no means true about amateur play, or sport practiced by the general public. The majority of States, at least those of the developed world, drive and favor sport as an integral part of the well-being and quality of life of their citizens. It also seems that no one would negate this function, but rather the contrary; it is one of the services inherent to the Welfare State to facilitate and promote citizens' practice of some sport activities (Cazorla 1979; 210).

Secondly, from a leftist theoretical standpoint (although not only from this perspective), it has often been pointed out that the purported "neutrality" of sport has never actually been born out in practice.

"Official sport ideology constantly affirms not only the true apoliticization of the sport movement, but also the apolitical will of its leaders. But the effective reality of the institutional practice of sport shows that, on the contrary, sport is tightly interwoven with the politics and activities of the State" (Brohm 1982; 189).

Brohm himself, quoting MacIntosh, highlights that the politicization of sport is not a contemporary phenomenon; rather, ever since the first expressions of sport which hark back to classical Greece, sport was already being used for political purposes:

> The politicisation of sport has existed since the times of the ancient Olympic games in which cities rivalled each other for prestige in a sort of sporting potlatch . . . it is doubtful that the non-political nature of sport has ever been true since the very moment in which Pelops conquered Oenomaus in the chariot race and took the queen as his reward (Brohm 1982; 190).

In any case, the relationship between sport and politics can be divided into three sections. To start off, there are some politics internal to sport, that is, the struggles and conflicts produced between sport clubs, federations, and organizations with the aim of gaining positions of power. Next, sport has been used for foreign policy purposes, and finally, sport has been used to influence domestic policy goals. In spite of the relevance that the first section may have, it will not be the object of study here, as I will focus my analysis on the other two. In a certain sense, this political use of sport can be seen as a manifestation of political nationalism expressed at the domestic or foreign policy level. Thus, I will take sporting nationalism to be the set of measures in support of athletes, teams, or national teams, both by political authorities as well as by the interests of a country. In the following, I will further examine the different degrees of development of sporting nationalism, which can directly affect its political-moral justification. In some cases, sporting nationalism bolsters competitiveness between nations in an undeserving and exaggerated fashion, leading to violent acts and vandalism by fans or to athletes playing a dirty game. Some authors even claim that it can be linked to political genocide. Given this type of link, sporting nationalism has moral relevance and calls into question the necessity of continuing sporting competitions between States.

THE USE OF SPORTS FOR FOREIGN POLICY GOALS: SPORTING NATIONALISM

Beyond the assertion of some authors that the political use of sport has always existed, it is perhaps certain this political use of sport is greatest when States decide to create national teams to compete against each other. The process culminated with the arrival on the scene of the Olympic Games at the close of the nineteenth century. Despite the Olympic Games being presented as an international calling, within a framework of understanding between the countries involved, what is certain is that from that moment on, the athletes do not display their physical skills only to beat personal bests or defeat a rival. Now they also "fight," they "represent" the State of which they are citizens, and for this reason they are bearers of all the standards, virtues, and values that are attributed to a nation, as well as the hallmarks of their defects and especially their pending debts, their affronts, and their historical enemies from other countries. In this way, they are exalted as heroes when they win against traditional rivals, but they are vilified, or even despised when they are defeated on this new battlefield, whether this is the football pitch, the running track or the basketball court. Athletes have ended up adopting, on many occasions, traits that have been promoted by nationalistic discourse, with a certain militaristic slant, an extreme or irrational sense of pride and a bellicose attitude toward rivals.

The result is that nowadays, sport and nationalism are probably two of the most exciting and passionate phenomena in the contemporary world. They are known to be so intertwined that it is not uncommon to identify certain national sports as the property of the country or find that they, in some way, represent the national character. This is how the former British prime minister thought when he pointed to cricket as the quintessential game of the English nation (Bairner 2001; xi).

Nationalism and sport inspire great reverence and devotion from fans so that members of the nation feel that being represented by the team on the field of football, rugby, or cricket constitutes a core element of their personal identity. This is simply put by Alan Sharpe, describing the experience of watching Scotland play football: "For a time before, throughout and after (the match) I have the feeling that my personal worth is bound up with Scotland's success or failure" (Allison 2000; 345).

On one hand, it is clear that from the influence between sport and nationalism, the phenomenon of chauvinism has cropped up, as have outbreaks of violence. However, perhaps the greater problem with the link between nationalism and sport is that they have generated vandalistic behavior among fans, so that confrontations in sport between rival nations have produced acts of violence. One author has even gone as far as to suggest a relationship between nationalism in sport and genocide (Gomberg 2000).

The relationship between sport and nationalism is not easy to describe, and it is even less easy to establish criteria that would allow making conclusive judgments about its positive and negative effects. This is firstly so because there is no general rule according to which it can be established that all nation-states "live" or utilize sport in the same way or to the same extent in order to obtain some type of interest or end goal. There are very nationalistic States, while others are less so; still others make reasonable use of sporting nationalism. For example, Germany has been a country which since the end of World War II has had "light" nationalist manifestations, so much so that citizens expressed surprise at seeing flags in the streets during a 2006 World Cup celebration. And there are States who are quite nationalistic but have correctly used sport, while there are those that have not done so, as will be seen below.

The vision of the relationship between nationalism and sport will depend on the previously established judgment on nationalism and on sport itself. The end goals of nationalism and sport appear to be profoundly linked in that sport has become a vehicle for expressing nationalistic sentiments. In this way, it is not uncommon for political authorities of States to use it for their "nation building" purposes. It is also used to give wings in other cases to separatist movements.

Neither is it uncommon for sport to be used to foster or increase cohesive internal resistance, or to shore up the government in moments of difficulty or crisis. There is no shortage of examples: Argentina during the 1978 World Cup, or the rise of Eastern European countries in sport as a propaganda mechanism abroad. Even more: there was a football match which started the war between Honduras and El Salvador in 1969. There are more cases in which it would be more reasonable to infer that national sport had helped a nationalist cause than that it has hindered or made no difference at all (Allison 2000; 352). But it seems also true that there is no reason to suppose a normal, let alone universal, relation between national sport and political nationalism. As Allison points out, "Each case is different and context is all-important . . . many of the five million English people with Irish family connections support the Irish rugby team or the Republic of Ireland football team. But this does not necessarily imply support for Irish unification" (Allison 2000; 351).

On the other hand, examining the issues between sport and nationalism requires previously establishing the significance of the term nationalism and, in this way, clarifying the influential relationships between both variables.

It is not easy to clearly delineate the concept of nationalism, nor does there exist a unanimous valuation of it. "Nation and the concepts derived from it are among the most shifting and elusive in the entire study of society, not least because they arouse so much emotion" (Allison 2000; 349).

In effect, the traits that define this phenomenon are far from being clarified. In spite of mentioning characteristics like language, culture, religion and traditions, it is clear that it has not been possible to establish one convincing way of identifying a nation. On the other hand, there is no one unique way of manifesting "nationalism"; its defenders sometimes speak of political and cultural nationalism (Margalit 1997; 115), or of conservative, liberal, atavistic, modern, exclusionary, resistance nationalism and so on (Feinberg 1997; 105). Those who defend the virtues of nationalism appeal to the fact that nationalism satisfies the profound need of human beings to belong to a society that allows them to form a complete life. This was the principle argument of Herder. Nowadays, it is Charles Taylor who highlights, on one hand, that a relationship should not be established between nationalism and atavism:

> Nationalism, I have wanted to say, can't be understood as an atavistic reaction. It is a quintessentially modern phenomenon (Taylor 1997; 43).

On the other hand, he argues that nationalism constitutes a legitimate reaction in the face of threats to dignity:

> I am trying to identify the source of the modern nationalism turn, the refusal—at first among elites—of incorporation by the metropolitan culture, as a recognition of the need for difference but felt existentially as a challenge, not just as a matter of valuable common good to be created but also viscerally as a matter of dignity, in which one's self-worth is engaged. This is what gives nationalism its emotive power. This is what places it so frequently in the register of pride and humiliation (Kim-McMahan 1997; 45).

In effect, nationalism creates clearly favorable conditions for some virtues such as loyalty, compromise and personal sacrifice. Consequently, these authors do not consider it necessarily as something negative that a partial attitude faced with opposing interests of people or collectives from nationalism is derived. For MacIntyre (1984), patriotism establishes how one should act according to the majority conceptions of the good life in the society where an individual lives, independently of whether that leads to committing unjust actions against other nations. From more moderate perspectives, it is held that when it is not possible to accommodate the interests of two nations that are in conflict over a matter, then national interests shall have the right to choose their own path.

Nevertheless, there are less optimistic perspectives about the presumed virtues of nationalism. Walter Feinberg points out that nationalism acts as a partially moral perspective since it leads individuals to have more favorable, if not clearly discriminatory, attitudes to their fellow citizens than to citizens of other nations.

> The rise of nationalism involves the development of a specific form of collective identity, one that is seen to originate in a shared language, culture and historical experience. People who expresses particular nationalist sentiments usually hold that they are obliged to favor conationals and that their nation has a right to recognition by others. This recognition entails, among other things, acceptance by outsiders of the special moral obligation that people within the nation have to one another (Feinberg 1997; 66).

In addition, nationalism assumes that it is correct to make all those decisions or actions that favor a sense of belonging of the members of a national community (McMahan 1997; 161). Bolstering a collective identity is something that is correct, in spite of the fact that it can occasionally entail disregarding the interests of other individuals or groups inserted in the same community as well as the interests of other different communities or nations. In addition to that, the demand for loyalty to the group is also characteristic of nationalism. In this sense, nationalism is opposed to universalism, seen as a concept that considers individuals should be treated in a certain way, independent from their belonging to a certain nation. In short, within the field of sport, nationalism involves granting favorable treatment to athletes of one's own nation.

As has been previously pointed out from a leftist point of view, the politicisation of sport and specifically the establishment of competition between nations, in the emblematic manner of the Olympic Games, leads States to consolidate their national identity or improve their national prestige in the concert of countries. In effect, the great international sporting events are the occasion for governments of most countries to take action in order to increase nationalist fervor. As Brohm points out:

> Countries utilize shields and emblems to symbolically identify and distinguish themselves as they did in the Middle Ages, when France takes the cock to the stature of the heart, England, a rose. . . . These coats of arms and emblems then act as a symbol of union that is hoisted amongst shouts of support in the stadiums. These fetish objects are considerably important in sport because they allow a partial object to be identified through sometimes acts as a symbolic fetish (Brohm 1982; 198).

The language of the media is a perfect reflection of the extent of nationalistic chauvinism with headlines that extol the virtues of patriotic athletes and personify the national teams with the feature itself, as happened over the course of several decades of "the fury" with the Spanish national football team. Athletes in these competitions act as soldiers fighting in missions on foreign territory in defence of national interests, which are represented by the victory hoisted high on the national flag. As Brohm points out,

> Sport offers a considerable outlet for national identification. In effect, sport allows a great social body to identify with the symbolic sporting body of the nation (Brohm 1982; 196).

In the context of the Cold War between Western capitalist countries and communists of Eastern Europe, the politicization of sport reached its peak. Athletes were turned into ambassadors and soldiers who defended not only their valor but also their country's ideology, political regime and way of life.

Other authors have unmasked the negative face of nationalism due to the fact that it is a powerfully dangerous force. For example, Berlin warns that besides having valuable aspects, political nationalism leads to thinking that others are "inferior" by nature. In this sense, the psychological feeling of national superiority puts nationalism on a continuum whose extreme is fascism. As Berlin says: "If Fascism is the extreme expression of this attitude, all nationalism is infected by it to some degree" (Berlin quoted by Margalit 1997; 85).

Tamburrini points in a similar direction when he notes:

> Thus MacIntyre's version of patriotism is deplorable simply because it sanctions conducts that are harmful to other people based on irrelevant foundations. The fact that a group of people do not belong to our community cannot be a reason to justify harming them. This critique also affects Nathanson's modified patriotic position (Tamburrini 2000; 93).

Linked to these theoretical objections, other authors have highlighted the connection between nationalism, violence and bad sporting practice. One of the principle critiques on nationalism and its expression in sport is that it can generate tension amongst competing athletes and fans from different countries, and even promote outbreaks of violence.

Along these lines, N. Dixon points to sporting nationalism as something that often contributes to fans of a national team (or individuals on a national team) acting in unsportsmanlike ways to the detriment of rival athletes and it can, on occasions, foster violence:

> A tiny minority of English soccer fans sometimes rampage through foreign cities where the national team is playing, destroying property and attacking opposing fans. Even when no physical violence occurs, racial and ethnic abuse of players for rival nations' teams is an all-too-common excess of nationalism. And chauvinistic fans can deliberately or inadvertently interfere with the performance of athletes from other countries, for instance by yelling as a player is about to serve a tennis ball or hit a putt, or—as happened during the 1996 Olympics held in Atlanta—inappropriately chanting support for the United States team during the routines of a foreign gymnast. . . . What all of these instances

of inappropriate, excessive patriotism have in common is a simple lack
of moral regard for athletes, coaches, and other people from rival countries (Dixon 2000; 75).

There have been several counter critiques to these objections linking
sporting nationalism and violence. In the first place, sport rivalry that
leads to bad practices and violence between the athletes themselves and
the fans is not exclusive to nationalist confrontations. Rather, this happens quite frequently at the domestic level. It is clear that the level of
sport rivalry has, on many occasions, been of a greater degree between
non-national teams, but rather ones that represent a city or a region. In
some cases, such rivalries have been so histrionic, or worse, and equally
dangerous, as those that that spring from international enemies, given
that age-old hatred has generated and deepened between different (opposing) fans. The tensions between opposing teams may be of differing
types: cultural, historic, political, or territorial reasons. It is almost unnecessary to point out the rivalry in the football arena between Real Madrid
and FC Barcelona for political-territorial reasons. Also well-known is the
rivalry between the "barras bravas" (hooligans) in Argentine club football in general, especially those of Boca and River. (In 2008, there were
thirty-eight injuries during the Argentine football season.) Others are po-
litical-classist type conflicts, such as those that take place in Israel between the so-called "Hapoel" (meaning "worker") teams, since these
usually come from labor unions. Facing these working class teams are the
"Beitar" teams which are closer to the political right (Reguera 2008; 82).
Other variations that have given rise to greater passion and violence have
been the opposition that may occur between teams linked to a certain
religion. Perhaps the most well-known examples are matches between
the Scottish teams Catholic Celtic and Protestant Glasgow Rangers.

Secondly, it has also been pointed out that sport in general, and more
precisely the national representation of athletes and sport teams, plays a
primordial role as an escape valve for more extreme nationalistic attitudes and sentiments. It is obvious that it would be preferable that those
sentiments against other nations did not exist, but we live in a world
where national hatred does still exist. From a realistic point of view, sport
serves as an escape valve for the bellicose passions that could have nefari-
ous consequences if there were no other way to express these feelings. In
this way, during a match or a competition, fans have the "freedom," or
even the "right" to unleash prejudices and hostility on athletes and fans
from other countries and to then return to everyday routines after letting
go of these bellicose passions. It is preferable then, that manifestations of
public disorder or violence take place in closed and controlled places, like
stadiums. It is also better that they do not happen suddenly, or that they
become difficult to control (Tamburrini 2000).

But perhaps the main counter criticism lies in that the phenomena mentioned above, which may seem to be caused by sporting nationalism, but may be caused by other, deeper factors. That is, the cause of undesirable behavior and violence that is manifested in stadiums does not have its roots in sport itself or in national teams, but in other factors like poverty, marginalization, social oppression or in the festering of past nationalistic insults. For all these reasons, it would be unfair to attribute the cause of violence or the bellicose nature of fans to sporting nationalism.

Even though the counterarguments are quite solid, there still remains some question regarding the legitimacy of sporting nationalism. Perhaps the focus in analyzing this link between two variables should not be from the perspective that the former causes the latter, but rather if the former contributes to the expression of the latter. This is the position of Tamburrini, summarized below, who highlights that sporting nationalism contributes to violence and vandalism:

> Even when such phenomena like vandalism and violence are present in national sport competitions, in any case sportive nationalism bolsters these phenomena. Besides, it could be affirmed that even if vandalism is not generated in sport arenas, stadiums constitute an appropriate stage for their manifestation. Then, even though it is not the cause of violence in spectators, the sport may be equally guilty of facilitating its de facto existence and of increasing its magnitude (Tamburrini 2000; 94).

Later, he reiterates the argument:

> Vandalism is a problem for sport, and the national sentiments associated with international sport competitions contribute to increasing the number and magnitude of expressions of vandalistic violence (Tamburrini 2000; 95).

However, this argument lacks logical coherence, given that it does not explain the necessary relationship between sporting nationalism and vandalism. It seems rather an empirical-probabilistic argument that should be founded on evidence and concrete examples. Over the course of a year, there are countless international sport competitions where countries from different continents, traditions, cultures, and ideologies, etc., face off, and it is rather uncommon or practically non-existent to hear that such competitions result in vandalism. All things considered, it is similar to the argument against pornography; the argument highlights that the number of crimes committed by men against women would rise, given the position of subordination that women tend to face in pornography. But there is not proof that this is the case. That is partially due to the fact that spectators are capable of distinguishing fiction from reality. This, it seems to me, is what happens when fans watch an international competition, after which a great measure of the hate and rivalry that could have manifested itself in the stadium disappears. Only if it were the case that a causal relationship could be established would it be necessary to take counter measures against the existence of international sport competitions.

In contrast, the positive elements that tend to go hand-in-hand with such events are palpable: they are usually full of spectators' excitement and passion, which contributes to the joy of the experience. Tamburrini himself takes up this argument in answer to the question of whether nationalism works to the detriment of sport. His answer is that it does not work to the detriment of sport, but rather, it even contributes to increasing the technical skill of the athletes:

> Far from ruining sport competitions, increased antagonism contributes to making them more exciting. This puts greater demands on the sport activity. It requires greater sacrifices and efforts to be made by the athletes. But this will be compensated for by the fact that the public will more greatly enjoy the tension that characterises more combative competitions. The rise in competitiveness could give rise to a better technical level in different sports. In this way, not only the hedonistic experience of the public could be increased, the quality of the game itself could rise as a consequence of more combative confrontations between athletes (Tamburrini 2000; 82).

In sum, having examined the pros and cons of sporting nationalism in terms of foreign policy, it seems to me that there are not sufficient reasons to establish a causal link or to claim that it contributes to violence. It follows that there do not seem to me to be any moral or political reasons to eliminate international competitions or to even substantially change their current structure. Neither should sporting nationalism be perceived to have provoked a considerable increase in non-sportsman-like behavior in competitions, if these are compared to the behavior in domestic competitions. Nevertheless, this conclusion is conditional on the assumption that the degree of sporting nationalism manifested between States will continue at current levels. If an increase in violence or in unsportsman-like practice, as a result of sporting nationalism, is observed, there may be reason to reopen this debate. In this sense, it would be possible to establish a type of sporting nationalism "thermometer" according to which the degree that it contributes to vandalism, violence, or bad sport practice is observed. Importing a distinction made by J. Parry (1998; 207) regarding the adjacent topic of violence in sport, among assertive, aggressive and violent behaviors themselves, in the same way a classification of sporting nationalism can be made according to three degrees. Before elaborating on this classification, I will foreshadow my eventual critique, warning that it is a vaguely limited classification since it will not be easy, in some cases, to distinguish between aggressive and violent behavior, such as the case of inciting hatred, which a media outlet may perform against a rival.

Assertive sporting nationalism would correspond to an active society in whose actions there is a positive sense of affirmation or insistence on individuals' rights, or even the protection and vindication of the collective identity itself. It seems clear that there is no moral reproach for this type of nationalistic expression which attempts to reaffirm the sense of community without necessarily confronting rivals. Said another way, this nationalistic expression constructs its own identity without undermining that of other communities.

Aggressive sporting nationalism comprises behavior that implies some degree of force and some type of vigorous, offensive and active attitude; that of striking first. As Parry himself points out, its moral acceptability may depend on the context. In the competitive sport arena, aggression is largely accepted, but it does not seem clear if this should be the case in other non-sport environments. As was seen in the last chapter, aggression is not physically expressed; rather it tends to be seen in verbal, psychological, economic or other types of manifestations. While a variety of behaviors could fit the definition, some of them are clearly unacceptable, such as, for example, disdaining and humiliating a player or the society (or nation) of a rival team, or provoking errors in their performance instead of cheering on one's own team. If this were the case, the country, whether it is the government or the fans, would be demonstrating unjustified aggressive sporting nationalism, and for that reason, could be censured. In contrast, an example of aggressive behavior that would not necessarily be reproachable is the case of a State investing effort and money in improving the quality of its national teams in order to obtain better future results, as long as it is not an exaggerated investment that stopped the State from fulfilling its more relevant social objectives. I will return to this point later on.

Lastly, violent sporting nationalism would involve the intention to physically harm another country. If violence in sport paradigmatically involves inflicting some physical injury on the rise, in the realm of nationalism, it would imply an intentional act by a country (government or fans) that is part of a chain reaction resulting in the physical injury of athletes, fans, or goods of another country. Of course, this characterization suffers from a certain degree of indeterminacy, which makes it quite difficult to prove when a government or fan has acted violently towards a rival country, a difficulty that would render it virtually impossible to define and recognize after the fact because the actions that have produced harm were premeditated, a topic that a virtual deluge of material has been written about in criminal law. But this does not render it impossible that there may be clear cases.

THE USE OF SPORT FOR DOMESTIC POLICY GOALS

One of the classic objections to the phenomena of sport is that it constitutes "the drug of the people," that is, sport is used by the state as a
political diversion factor to distract the citizenry from political, social,
and economic matters that are truly relevant to the individual's or class's
interest (Brohm 1982; 214). This critique does not come exclusively from
the left; it is taken up by authors of differing political ties who highlight
other possible uses of sport. For example, Cazorla (1979; 5) distinguishes
between two types of uses of sport by politics according to the degree in
which it is used: sporadic or systematic. In the first case, the use of sport
would basically have the goal of distracting society from some political
happening. In the second, the aim would be to inculcate society with a
special ideology or vision of the world. Examples of this type can be
found in fascist or communist uses of sport. Another example of this
political use of sport, according to Cazorla, was the use that Franco's
government gave to sport after 1939 under the command of Falange:
"having the management of sport in the hands of one sole party, its
guidelines, objectives, teachings and directives were born by and from
inside the party and, we shall say, for the party. Confiding one body with
so much political significance, the management of sport purported to
shape those who were most interested in it, the youth, joining itself with
the Movimiento Nacional candidates" (Cazorla 1979; 218). The consequence of this policy, according to the same author, was that the main
concern was "bolstering the sport-show (more than) bolstering sport for
all . . . The reason for that is obvious. With the predominance of the sport-
show the citizenry was 'drugged,' its alienation facilitated the separation
from the political stage, the laissez-fair politics" (Cazorla 1979; 219). It
seems clear that this use of sport is illegitimate since it is used to strength-
en not only antidemocratic values but ones that are far removed from the
internal principles of the sporting phenomenon.

As for Tamburrini, he analyzes whether the abusive devotion to sport
matters by the State could also be considered harmful to citizens given
that it would contribute to distracting attention or effort relating to more
urgent socio-political matters. In order to proceed with an analytical
method of examining this issue, this author distinguishes between two
possible scenarios. Firstly, the political use of sport under normal political circumstances and in situations of political and social crises, a distinction that I will use with certain modifications beyond those that Tamburrini himself suggested.

THE POLITICAL USE OF SPORT UNDER NORMAL POLITICAL CIRCUMSTANCES

From the left, the use of sport has been criticized even when it is not highly politicized, as was seen in the systematic use of sport in the previous section. In effect, even when the political authority tries to keep sport in a neutral environment, it tends to be used for political ends. The first objection to how sport is used in States in capitalistic societies arises from the fact that it seems to be a neutral institution, one that is above all political contingencies and contradictions. This seemingly neutral attitude does nothing more than contribute to

> uncritically legitimizing the established social order which is represented as neutral and contradiction-free. This thesis of "political neutrality" is defended with beautiful unanimity by sport ideologies (Brohm 1982; 201).

This function of sport within the social framework is what Brohm calls the "positivist function of sport."

The second major critique of the sport phenomenon is that does not only legitimize the social, political and economic order of the society in which it is involved, it contributes with an additional integrative function that further stabilizes the capitalist system.

> Sport, through the discipline that it imposes, uncovers the need for rules, the benefits of free and organised effort. Through life in a team . . . it institutes respect for the legally established hierarchy as well as a sense of equality, solidarity and interdependence. It is indubitably an excellent way of learning about human relations and a remarkable school of socialisation. In this way, it can be appreciated that sport is conceived of a priori as a means of integration and adaptation of the individual (Brohm 1982; 206).

That is, sport socializes the future worker who has played sport since childhood and through this practice, the norms, order, discipline, and most of all, "an ideologically valued social model" are conveyed.

Faced with the conflicts of interest between classes that are produced and expressed in economic relationships, sport acts as a balm, given that it offers the opportunity for reconciliation and unity of individuals both in the practice of sport and in the support of teams and athletes playing for the country. Thus, sport acts as a social glue that unites millions of people under a common interest. By supporting a national team, citizens forget their economic, political and class differences. In the stadium or victory celebration afterwards, no differences are perceived or noteworthy. In this way, Brohm concludes that

> sport, due to the fact that it provides a show for the masses, which is tolerated and encouraged by the State, constitutes a spectacular politi-

cal manifestation and glorification of the established order (Brohm
1982; 208).

Nevertheless, these critiques miss part of the attractiveness and strength
of sport. We attend to the fact that along with other social happenings,
such as education, family, and means of communication, sport provides a
more effective social integration tool, if not the most effective one. On the
other hand, these mechanisms are instruments of integration whose work
must be evaluated according to the values and ideologies that they aim to
inculcate in the citizenry. It does not seem that sport should deserve the
same value judgment if the values that it entails and conveys are democratic or fascist. And it would seem that in advanced democratic societies,
the values that it promotes cannot be boiled down to only what Brohm
points to. There are also other noteworthy aspects to personalities and
collectives: solidarity, companionship, effort, demands on self, etc.

Even so, in normal democratic contexts there are authors who question if a certain manifestation of sporting discipline is legitimate. In this
regard, Tamburrini wonders if it is negative that fans of a nation like
Sweden (which enjoys a well-functioning society and is free of economic
and social needs) cheer for and support its football team at an international event. His answer is two-pronged. As long as there are no special
or pressing socio-economic problems that Swedes should attend to in
their own country, it does not seem that they should be embarrassed or
feel any kind of moral reproach for being interested in their national
sport teams. However, the issue is that outside the country there continue
to be problems with poverty and dictatorial regimes that Swedish citizens should pay attention to instead of devoting time to sport. For this
reason Tamburrini concludes:

> Given the richness, Swedes—unlike Nigerians—can alleviate much of
> the misery that still pesters the world. For this reason, although it is not
> negative (at least not directly) for the nation itself, the 1994 football
> celebration can be questioned, not for distracting efforts from pressing
> social matters in the country itself, but rather for not having completed
> active international aid abroad (Tamburrini 2000; 103).

However, this critique seems somewhat exaggerated as well as lacking in
precision. Regarding the first issue, the claim seems exaggerated given
that it is not the case that Swedish fans (or fans from countries with
similar economic levels) totally abandon their responsibility to aid the
Third World by putting their attention on the national team for a few
days per year. Citizens' interest in sport, which is concentrated for a brief
period of time, does not exclude managing one's deserved moral respon-
sibilities towards those on the planet who are less fortunate. With the
moral requirements that Tamburrini lays out, it seems that Swedes
would begin to see their situation as a "moral inferno." In terms of Tamburrini's second point about the specific moral demands, which ones

make it so countries cannot legitimately celebrate the victories of their teams? Where is the threshold between rich and poor countries? All things considered, there is no reason for "moral panic."

There is, however, another aspect of sporting nationalism that does seem questionable in more developed Western societies, an aspect that has not been the subject of great criticism. It is that many countries invest astronomical amounts of money in athletes, infrastructure, technology, and sport programs with a view to attaining better results on the international stage. This phenomenon is especially blatant in the Olympic Games. As it was pointed out elsewhere, Australia managed to secure fourth place in the overall medal count for the Athens Olympics thanks to enormous monetary investment by the government. It has been calculated that each medal cost $32 million. The question is if this is a legitimate manifestation of sporting nationalism. In my opinion, it is not. There are two reasons for this. In the first place, my objections stem from the unjustifiable increase in the already profound inequalities between athletes of different countries. If there was already a huge difference between Nigerian athletes, for example, and Australian ones, with enormous economic investments, these differences would be greater still and more questionable for the supposedly sought-after equality among athletes. In the second place, beyond specifically how much economic support a state should put into national team athletes for domestic and international competitions, it seems clear that the amounts invested by the Australian government for improving the athletes' facilities exceed what is reasonable for a democratic society that is concerned about global economic inequality. For this reason, this investment implies noncompliance with the moral obligations that developed countries have to less developed ones where many suffer from hunger and generalized poverty.

THE POLITICAL USE OF FORCE IN CRISIS POLITICAL SITUATIONS

Once again, leftist ideologies have raised especially virulent critiques on the role of sport in countries with precarious economic conditions. It is usual for sport to be taken advantage of by governments to provide a (false) outlet for the tensions and the misery of an impoverished population. In this way, the population is entertained with the success of the country's athletes instead of worrying about trying to reverse the socioeconomic situation in which they live, i.e., they are not concerned with carrying out policies conducive to eradicating the power of the elite and establishing economic measures that better meet the real needs of the population.

But a number of decades have already passed since Brohms first criticized underdeveloped countries for the role that sport played in political diversion as well as for being an honest-to-goodness "drug of the peo-

ple." In societies that suffer from the scourge of poverty, governments—
either deliberately or not—use sport as an escape valve for those members of the worst-off social groups and in this way avoid, albeit briefly,
their daily toil (Brohm 1982; 215). The examples that can be given are
both many and varied, but perhaps one of the most interesting is that of
the utilization of football by Brazil in the context of a few decades back,
when the economic situation of the country was not as buoyant as it is
nowadays.

Nevertheless, several objections have been targeted at this view of
sport as the "drug of the people." Tamburrini points to the following
reasons. In the first place, this vision of sport at the service of the spurious
interests of the government would deny the "poor" the right to enjoy and
celebrate victories of the national team. In the second place, it involves
exercising clearly unjustified paternalism: it would entail establishing
from the privileged perspective of rich countries what is allowed and
prohibited in countries with less economic development. In the third
place, there is no empirical evidence that demonstrates that there is a
relationship between sport victories and political passivity in those environments where more convincing restorative social action seems to be
needed. In effect, it is far from being proved that the most efficient way to
solve socio-economic problems is to contain happiness in the face of a
sporting event. As Tamburrini highlights: "The supposed link between
refraining from celebrating and securing political and social improvements is, to put it carefully, indirect and difficult to show." Besides, the
Argentine author highlights that there are empirical studies that demonstrate a correlation between practicing sport and socio-political involve-
ment; other studies also show a correlation between attending sporting
events and an increase in social participation and commitment. Although
these studies may not be irrefutable, they do at least cast doubt on the
opposing thesis regarding the relationship between celebrating sports
and political passivity.

However, as mentioned in the previous section, another manifestation
of sporting nationalism that deserves a different opinion would be that of
countries devoting huge sums of money to promoting elite sport when
the masses are hungry or are in a deplorable economic situation. Leaving
aside the undeniable difficulties faced in discerning borderline cases of
"poor" countries, there may be clear cases where the judgment would not
be subject to doubt. Even if it were the case that these investors could
assure victory in sport (obviously doubtful), which would cause the people to feel happy (albeit in passing), there would be no possible justification for such measures when basic needs for a considerable part of the
population are not met.

Another type of social-political situation where it would be feasible to
conclude that the government and the people are acting incorrectly in
celebrating sport victories is the situation in which celebrations take place

within a context of massive violations of human rights. Tamburrini refers to the political use of the 1978 World Cup in football, held in Argentina, by the military government that seized power in a coup d'état. At the same time that matches were being played throughout Argentina, hundreds of people were being held in centers of torture, and others were assassinated with impunity by the military and police forces following the orders of the dictatorial government. The situation became even more flagrant with the victory of the Argentine team. This win led to an explosion of widespread joy in the country . . . even while kidnapping, torture and deaths of innocent people were taking place. In such situations, Tamburrini highlights that he tends "to conclude that Argentines, assuming that they knew about the kidnappings and murders, acted incorrectly in joining the celebration sponsored by the regime. I base this intuition on the direct effect, almost concretely discernible, that a massive boycott of the celebration would have had on the political stability of the military government" (Tamburrini 1982; 105). However, it is not by any means easy to follow the criteria that Tamburrini preaches. As has been pointed out above, this criteria involves two choices according to whether there is certainty or not that the non-celebration of victories may affect the stability of the regime. However, on what grounds should these previsions be established? There do not seem to be any scientific measurements that could determine the probable effect of popular protests on government stability, which makes it difficult to set a criteria for judging when a society should legitimately express a certain sporting nationalism as a way to celebrate victories. I am of the opinion that it is never appropriate that a country, where widespread human rights violations are taking place, should celebrate a sport victory, like the celebration that took place in Argentina during the football World Cup. This is independent from the political policy considerations made, whether this action has repercussion on the stability of the non-democratic government or not.

CONCLUSIONS

Throughout this chapter I have analyzed different forms of the relationship between sport and nationalism. There is no doubt that, given the importance of sport in the collective imagination of our society, this phenomenon has been constantly utilized by the political elite. The question is if all manifestations of sporting nationalism are worthy of censure.

Regarding these effects, I have distinguished between the political use of sport at the international and domestic levels.

Concerning a State's use of foreign policy, I have argued that despite a liberal universalist perspective, it would be desirable that neither nations (or moral agents) existed, nor that they increased in number while we are living in this current context. A minimum expression of sporting nationalism cannot be morally rejected at this point.

In the case of using sport to meet domestic policy goals, I have also reached the conclusion that sport in democratic societies has no reason to necessarily be the "drug of the people." This should not prevent there from being certain socio-political situations in which excessive monetary investment by States is made in order to promote sport as an act of dubious morality for the practice of sport itself. This may give rise to further inequalities among athletes, and it entails a more efficient and fair distribution of economic resources in societies with great social inequalities.

SIX

Technologically Modified Athletes and the Challenges to Sport

The zeal humanity shows to improve our physical (or cognitive) qualities is both widespread and socially acceptable, and the technology used to achieve these effects is not, for the most part, a topic that is called into question. There are enhancements that make use of surgery, implants, or pharmaceutical products that are perfectly socially acceptable. This is the case, for example, that allows surgery, Botox, piercing or the use of appetite suppressants for cosmetic purposes. In the field of music, it is perfectly acceptable to take a beta blocker like propranolol to counteract a musician's trembling before a concert. On a daily basis, there are different types of substances that enhance our cognitive abilities or modify our character: alcohol, nicotine, caffeine, Ritalin, Modafinil and Prozac, to name but a few. There are even substances that can be acquired in pharmacies to improve sexual performance as in the famous case of Viagra.

However, recent decades have seen more profound changes to the relationship between human beings and technology: the development of genetics, robotics, cybernetics, nanotechnology, and biomedicine are making it possible to posit that in the future human beings will be able to genetically modify and clone themselves; they will be able to create hybrid beings or interact with computers or other components from within the human body itself. A transhuman world, in which human beings are not limited by constraints imposed by nature, in which they can experience whatever physical change with the goal of increasing their physical or mental capacity, is for some the Fukuyama case, the most dangerous idea that lies in wait for humanity (Fukuyama 2002). Nevertheless, it is possible that indeed there is no good reason for such moral panic, as these changes are unlikely to be obligatory, but rather will be performed on individuals who have the free will to choose them. And on the other hand, they are designed to improve human capabilities, that is, they will produce more intelligent individuals with a much longer life expectancy than the one that exists now. This optimistic point of view, however, cannot hide the fact that there will be difficulties to deal with throughout this process: establishing access criteria that respect equality of opportunity and ensuring that it is not only the elite of society that have access to such changes. Additionally, it will also be necessary to take measures to prevent inequality between enhanced (post-human) and natural (or simply human) beings from arising. MacNamee and Edwards also point out that the road to transhumanism can be a slippery slope that leads to experimenting on the most fragile and dangerous aspects of human nature (aggression, egotism, etc.), which is far from being morally acceptable (McNamee and Edwards 2006). In contrast, Savulescu is of the mind that a slippery slope will not necessarily be brought about; rather, he sees this as a process with a number of stages that will be adequately controlled through medical and scientific advancements in such a way that undesirable results will be avoided (Savulescu 2011).

In any case, sport is not at the margin of technological enhancement advances to physiological abilities; it will not be immune to those future changes engendered by technology, no matter how vague or nebulous they may seem to us now. Rather, they will probably be one of the social spheres where these transformations on the human body will be seen for the first time. Given the idiosyncrasies of athletes, their eagerness to reach new goals, their attraction to fame, the thirst for higher incomes and the like, it is more likely that they will be the "scouting party" that experiments first with this progress in genetics. Some authors, like Miah, point out that technological advancements currently applied to sport already make athletes that are post-human (Miah 2004).

Technology plays an increasingly important role in sport, not only for those sports in which the athlete uses a type of vehicle (motorcycling, cycling, etc.) where technological advances are continuous and of increasingly greater magnitude. But, if the technological advances that are achieved are generally part of the accessories used by athletes, they already constitute a problem for purists. When technology directly affects the human body, the doubts about its legitimacy are already significant.

Whether or not this distinction is worthy of discussion, the use of technology in sport can be carried out with distinct therapeutic or enhancement goals (Longman 2007, Miah 2004). The doubts about its legitimacy in sport arise when it is used for enhancement effects. It is then that this use becomes one of the core matters for sport authorities who must set the conditions regulating athletes' participation in different tests. Although these conditions may be realized in a different manner in the future, the three types of enhancement modifications that athletes could experiment in a not-so-distant future are: gene doping, implants in the body that would convert athletes into cyborgs, and the creation of hybrid beings and chimeras. Below, I will briefly paraphrase what each one of these changes could consist of in these three areas of technological advancement as applied to sport. In the following section, I will examine some of the problems that arise and, finally, I will highlight that perhaps there is no reason for the "moral panic" that some scholars forebode.

GENE DOPING AND SPORT

The human genome has been called the book of life because in contains all the basic information about what we call a human being. The decoding that took place a number of years ago (and that still continues today) has opened up the possibility of a wide range of possible genetic treatments as well as technologies that will be developed, both for enhancement and therapeutic purposes. And on a not-so-distant horizon is the ability to manipulate and design human beings with certain particular features or abilities which will make way for them to be called "transhumans" (Bostrom 2003). Other authors point out that genetic research could open the door not only to the possibility of providing therapy but also to make it able for human beings to be born with fewer illnesses, although this is a future marked by many variables. As the so-called "transhumans" may dream, genetic engineering can offer a future to those individuals who have the ability to choose their own destiny, and to stop being subject to its influence, or to the resolve to be influenced by the natural genetic lottery.[1] This kind of world would allow the human being to flourish beyond the limits imposed by Nature (Bostrom 2003).

The scientific and medical advances aimed at improving physical performance of humans in general and of athletes in particular have been exploring a variety of new methods, now having arrived at what is known as gene doping. This technique is understood as the introduction and subsequent expression of a transgene and the modification of the activity of an existing gene in order to obtain an additional physiological advantage. The World Anti-Doping Agency (WADA) defines gene doping in similar terms.

Scientists have pointed out that some gene candidates for gene doping, such as Erythropoietin (EPO), the insulin-like growth factor 1 (IGF-1), growth hormone (GH), and Hypoxia-inducible factors (HIFs), as well as Peroxisome proliferator-activated receptors alpha (PPAR-alpha). Each of these genes is linked to a specific enhanced type of performance whether it is the greater transfer of oxygen to muscles, the increase muscle mass or increase in height.

Genetic interventions can be of two distinct types based on the types of effects that they may have:

a) Somatic interventions: this type of treatment consists of cell-based intervention to modify the genome (the genetic structure) of already ex-

isting beings with a view to making them more resistant to certain illnesses or to improve their physical abilities.

This type of intervention has been applied in seed cultivation and
animal feed industries. Nonetheless, its use in human beings is still in the
initial stages of development. In the case of sport, this method could
involve an intervention to achieve better performances. It deals with
interventions, the aim of which is the modification of those genes linked
to physical performance (Erythropoietin, insulin-like growth factor 1,
growth hormone and hypoxia-inducible factors and peroxisome proliferator-activated receptors alpha are local in that they operate on somatic
cells. For this reason variations cannot be transmitted genetically to an
individual or his or her offspring.)

b) Germline genetic modifications: Here modifications are carried out
on the germline of cells (sperm, unfertilized eggs, or recently fertilized
embryos) to increase their metabolic capabilities and in this way to improve health or physical performance abilities. Given that much of the
basic structures of the human body are established at very early stages of
life, these modifications have to be realized before individuals are born
since most of these capabilities are determined prior to cellular development. In this way, the result of this type of genetic intervention will be
inheritable and can be transmitted from one generation to the next.

At the same time, two types of technical modifications can be distinguished in the germline. The first type takes place after in vitro fertilization (the development of an embryo before implantation) and entails the
genetic modification of fetal embryonic stem cells. These genetically
modified cells are introduced into blastocysts (a very early stage of the
embryo) in such a way that the germline genetic information of the future
individual is changed.

The other procedure includes cloning. The adult somatic cell is genetically engineered. Then the nucleus of the modified cell is inserted into an
egg without a nucleus, in this way simulating fertilization and generating
an embryo that has the genetic information of the initial adult plus the
added genetic modification. If the procedure is carried out correctly, an
embryo could be generated that had the new genetic information and
was, for example, free of genetic diseases that could be avoided with this
procedure. It is widely known that up until now these modification procedures have only been applied to animals, not human beings.

But in any case, whether it be through somatic or germline modifications, future gene trials could be possible and—if successful—could be
generalized. It is natural then to question whether the current ban on
these modifications is justified. And when faced with future possible
cases, what scenarios are possible with the different modifications and
their impact on sport performance? Not without abundant criticism
(Schneider 2000), Tännsjö and Tamburrini (2006) have claimed genetic
modification could well be a way to improve the natural disadvantage of

certain athletes, especially women when competing with men in certain athletic competitions. This point of view does not take into account whether women may be better genetically endowed in other sports or aspects of social life.

CYBORGS AND SPORT

Cyborg is a combination of the words "cybernetic" and "organism"; that is to say, they are organisms made up of biological elements and mechanical, electronic, or robotic devices, which are used primarily to better the capabilities of the biological organism through the use of technology.

The term was coined by Manfred E. Clynes and Nathan S. Kline in 1960. Reflecting on this type of creature, they concluded there was a need for a closer link between humans and machines at that historical juncture when scientific knowledge and technological development had progressed by leaps and bounds, especially in terms of space exploration.

The cyborgization of sport has occupied a role in medical and sport fields in recent years due to the fact that this issue calls into question the very foundations of contemporary sport, and consequently it gives rise to doubt about whether cyborg athletes should be able to take part in different athletic competitions, and if they are allowed, under what circumstances.

More specifically, this possibility generates inevitable ethical and legal questions. In this sense, the paradox that arises is that medical implants were invented with obvious therapeutic and restorative goals, which would improve the physical abilities of the (normally disabled) athletes. But, these enhancements can improve physical performance (Wolbring 2011b, Zettler 2009). On several occasions, the current state of technical development has led athletes with implants (cyborgs) to achieve better results or times than "regular" athletes. For this reason not only do these athletes claim that they should be allowed to take part in competitions for disabled athletes, but they should not be excluded from competitions for normal athletes (Dvorsky 2008). This is the case of the South African paralympic athlete Oscar Pistorius, who has reached great notoriety and whose claims have shaken even the most solid foundations of elite sport. His case, as an example of cyborgization of sport, makes it patently clear that the arguments both for and against the participation of these cyborg athletes in competitions for athletes who are not disabled must be further clarified.

GENETICALLY MODIFIED, HYBRID, AND CHIMERA ATHLETES

While it may seem that the existence of genetic enhancements and cyborg products is just around the corner, the production of hybrids and artificial chimeras is far from being feasible. Currently no hybrid humans or chimeras between species exist. For this reason, I intend to show in this section that it is simply a possibility. Nevertheless, this topic deserves to be brought forward and philosophically discussed as a challenge to sports ethics.

Natural hybrids in the animal kingdom have existed for years, as in the case of the mule—offspring of a male donkey and a mare or a stallion and a female donkey, the goat-sheep hybrid, the liger—the lion-tiger hybrid, or the zebroid—the cross between a zebra and a donkey. With the rapid development of science, hybrids could be created artificially and controlled by human beings. In actuality, what has been posited as a possibility are hybrids with human elements. They would be creating "new" beings whose ontological status would be, in short, ex novo or completely novel (De Miguel 2011, Savulescu 2011).

Chimeras are organisms that have genetic material at the cellular level that comes from two or more distinct organisms. Experiments designed to create artificial chimeras in the animal kingdom have been taking place for several decades. Ten years ago, a research team extracted tiny parts of the brain of a quail fetus and then introduced them into the brain of chicken fetuses. As a result, the chicks were born with quail features, such as warbling and head bobbing. But the potential to create chimeras with human elements does not seem impossible for some researchers. As Savulescu points out (Savulescu 2011), Irving Weissman—a specialist in chimera investigation—aspires to create rats completely out of human brain tissue.

Genetically modified organisms are those that have had a gene added to them; they are beings belonging to a given species, but they have been modified by introducing biological elements that belong to another. Here the driving question is to determine which species the modified beings belong to. Two examples can be found in ANDi, a rhesus monkey, and Alba, a rabbit, both of whom have the green fluorescent protein gene of a jellyfish incorporated into their DNA. Other than this, these animals are perfectly healthy and normal, the only odd thing being their fluorescent green glow. Recently, scientists have introduced a similar jellyfish gene into a human embryo, making it fluorescent. The embryo was destroyed, but if it had been carried to term, it would have produced a fluorescent human being (Savulescu 2011).

Although we have not yet encountered beings with these features, the ethical debates that arise from the new possibility to create beings with elements of humans themselves and of other animals are highly complex and cannot be treated in this context. As Savulescu points out, "It is not clear at present to which species chimeras would belong, and therefore nor which regulations and laws would apply, which potentially relevant moral abilities they would have, or in what sense these are relevant for them to be used in a certain way" (Savulescu 2011). By way of advocating for chimeras, Savulescu indicates that they could aid in creating species resistant to illnesses, they could provide useful products to humans, and they could also be used in xenotransplantation (transplants of tissue, cells, and organs from one species to another). Whether or not these matters are worthy of discussion (and some scientists negate that they are possible in the short or medium term), the issue of interest to sport is what may possibly occur in the future if beings with this type of enhanced physical characteristics, such as sight, are created. What should happen if they intend to take part in athletic competitions? As is the case with hermaphrodites and transsexuals, questions could arise about assigning them to a type of competition with normal athletes or creating a new competitive arena for them.

REGULATORY PROBLEMS

The three cases examined highlight some of the problems that sport authorities will have to deal with in the future given that these enhancements will produce athletes with better potential physical abilities, leading to the conclusion that modified athletes would have the upper hand when compared to "normal" athletes. What should be done? Should these advantages be considered something similar to doping and then be banned from participating in competitions as is now the case? Or rather, should they be able to compete head-to-head with normal athletes? Or should specific competitions be created for them only?

Experts in philosophy and ethics in sport have offered a variety of opinions and perspectives on the validity of increased sport performance as caused by gene doping, the increase in mechanical implants in athletes' bodies and the possible development of hybrid and chimera athletes. Much like the objections raised to doping, the reasons informing objections to the technological interventions in sport can be categorized into three main areas: 1) they affect the spirit of the sport, especially the equality among athletes; 2) they may eventually cause health problems; and 3) they dehumanize the sport. But to these objections, a fourth must be added: 4) they represent an aesthetic problem.

THE PROBLEM OF INEQUALITY

This first critique is commonly directed at conventional doping. According to it, physical improvement would be exaggerated in such a way that equality among athletes would no longer exist. But, as I have already pointed out, this critique provides a caricature of what the impact of these technologies would be in the playing of sports rather than a description of the actual circumstances. At least in its current state of affairs, technology has not advanced to such an extent that it would be able to create athletes who are vastly superior to "organic" ones. Athletes will have to continue training and making sacrifices to finally achieve good performance in the sport arena. Technology only offers a slight difference to times or goals achieved. Therefore, it follows that the athlete who relies on the miraculous results of a little pill and stops training could hardly be part of the elite.

In fact, the equality potentially produced as a result of the generalizing of these new treatments would lead to a situation in which effort, dedication and sacrifice would become more decisive factors in the practice of sports to a greater extent than they are today. Given that athletes would not be as different from each other with regard to their physical abilities, victory in a competition would depend on other factors[2]: the creative features of the athlete, his excellence of character, his technical decisions or his ability to take risks. Success in sport would not be left to random circumstances related to an individual's natural genetic lottery or the economic power of the country where the athlete is born. Being born endowed with a certain talent or in a rich country is completely random, and it may be possible to find moral reasons for compensating for these undeserved advantages.

The question then becomes what should be done if, in the future, these improvements to physical performance no longer qualify as normal, but rather become transhuman improvements (Tännsjö 2009)? By analyzing the extent of a treatment, it is feasible to distinguish between therapeutic, enhancement, and transhuman effects. A therapeutic effect would be one that repairs a body to more or less match its state previous to an illness. An enhancement effect would be one that would allow for an increase in natural human potential within the typical human realm, e.g., increasing an individual's IQ from 100 to 104. A transhuman effect would be superhuman improvement, that is, the increase of a person's abilities beyond the characteristic scope of the human species, e.g., increasing an individual's IQ from 100 to 200.

In this last case, it would seem reasonable to establish segregated competitions. In the same way there is justification for setting up segregated competitions based on age, weight, or sex. More than enough reasons could be given to create competitions for those individuals (whether or not they are genetically modified, cyborgs, or chimeras) that had superhuman physical abilities. It is obvious that we are unaware of the possible effects that these competitions could have on traditional favorites. Would they draw the attention of sports' traditional fan base, or would they remain in the background? In any case, there is no reason to impede the establishment of tests and competitions for these new athletes.

THE PROBLEM OF PROTECTION OF HEALTH

Regarding this second objection, to how technology could affect health, it has been pointed out that technology has not yet reached a point in development where it would produce consequences that are detrimental to health. In this way, it is suggested that cyborg sports with their improved technology would put the security and health of an athlete at grave risk due to the lack of knowledge of the long-term consequences of modifications to the human body. In effect, artificial implants on the human body may produce unpredictable consequences. In effect, in some cases long-term and chronic damage has been detected.

The case of gene doping presents a special particularity. Culbertson (2009) states that a prudent attitude is essential when faced with the future developments of genetic technology applied to sport, especially germline treatments. In his opinion, when the time comes that those treatments are feasible, the unpredictable nature of long-term genetic enhancement must be taken very seriously. This entails provisionally calling into question the arguments in favor of genetic enhancement.

In effect, we cannot be sure that we will be able to accurately predict the result of changes to the germline. We do not know if those changes will conform to the expectations based on past experiments. Put another way, the main issue at hand is that we lack sufficient information and are consequently not in a position to predict the results.

Culbertson attempts to graphically demonstrate the unpredictable nature of the results to germline therapy by comparing how this therapy can be used as applied to a "normal" case such as cystic fibrosis, a disease that results from a defective gene (and not the complex interaction of several genes) which is possible to replace.

Unlike traditional doping, gene transfer technology is still in the experimental stage of development. Despite all the investments that have been made, genetic engineering is still just at the incipient stages. While it has seen remarkable advances, there are failures that call into question whether it is ready to be applied generally or systematically to a population. Of special concern is the problem that certain methods of gene transfer are complex and irreversible and consequently the complications that might occur would have no solution after the fact. Scientists are just now starting to analyze and understand the very interaction of genes and the interactions between genes and the environment. The development of cancer is a known risk to genetic manipulation. The unexpected problems that may crop up in the development of new therapies could degenerate into adverse answers with respect to the predicted consequences. Even if the insertion of a gene is successful, there can still be risks associated with the expression of the gene, as can be seen in the incidents of polycythemia and anemia in primates that were used in animal experiments. In another experiment with the mice known as NR2B, or "Doogies," improved memory was accompanied by greater sensitivity to certain types of pain.

Given these considerations based on the prudence that should be taken when carrying out scientific research on gene manipulation applied to athletes who want to improve their performance, Schneider and Rupert conclude the following:

> For these reasons, one could argue that athletes cannot make an informed decision to "gene dope" (nor could a trained geneticist for that matter) as there simply is no information, on either the probability or magnitude of potential adverse effects (especially in the long term) or, perhaps more importantly from the athlete's perspective, the actual ergogenic benefits of the treatment. With the available evidence, this particular aspect of the argument from harm to users is the only one that is availing (Schneider and Rupert 2009; 196).

In short, given the eventual harm that could come to future progeny, it can be argued that measures should be taken to prevent germline doping from taking place given the fact that research is still in a very beginning stage and due to the unknown nature of the eventual possible negative effects that they may have on health. It follows that athletes are not fully disclosed on the potential harmful health consequences that genetic enhancements could have. In effect, given that future possibilities are the topic of discussion, we know very little about its potential effects and what could stem from these germline treatments.

It follows that, save these cases where third-party interests are at stake or where there is incomplete knowledge on the effects on medical and scientific treatments on an athlete's body, I believe it is opportune to respect the autonomy of the individual who decides to undergo an intervention to improve his sport performance. Despite the fact that athletes may be running the risk of negatively affecting their own health, athletes—just as any other autonomous citizens—are capable of deciding their own life plan, even if this implies a health risk. A ban would be an example of unjustified paternalism.

THE PROBLEM OF DEHUMANIZATION OF SPORT

The third objection deals with ethical matters: the "dehumanization" of sport (Hoberman 1992), given that it reduces the scope of an element that has been considered part and parcel of a fair competition. As Simon points out, athletes' extensive use of physical performance enhancement techniques may lead to a situation in which "we are incapable of identifying the original 'I' whose performance we want to improve" (Simon 1993).

There are several objections to the use of genetic technology, and particularly to its use in sport, but the principle objection is one that implies that our humanity is threatened. The problem here is with the characterization of "humanity" (Savulescu 2011). On some occasions, human beings as moral agents have been identified by belonging to the human species; on others, by their ability to feel. But perhaps currently the most widespread conception of "humanity" resides in the possession of superior cognitive abilities such as rationality, autonomy, consciousness, and self-consciousness. If this conception is adopted, it does not in any way seem that technologically modified athletes (at least to a certain point) lose their humanity: they reflect and feel, they are self-conscious and they can establish future life plans.

One variant of this criticism comes from Michael Sandel, who expresses the fear that human beings are playing God and are going against Nature (Sandel 2007). Leaving aside the religious interpretation in the sense that the concern is that humans literally usurp the role of a superior being, we will centre our analysis on the secular interpretation, the main concern that humans may not recognize their own limitations. To put it another way, they express "hubris," an exaggerated self-pride in their abilities as natural beings.

But the answer to this fear is that

> "the history of humanity has been one of modifying the world and life for good reasons. The natural state of humans would be a life 'nasty, brutish and short,' as Hobbes saw it, without many improvements that involved modifying the world. Vaccination, antibiotics and nearly all of medicine involve powerful interventions. The objection that we would be playing God is only valid as a caution against premature or ill-informed actions, to which no doubt humans are predisposed" (Savulescu 2011; 663).

For authors who declare that they are in favor of a "pure" sport, the appearance of cyborgs, in any of their manifestations whether they are slight or more extreme in their modifications, calls into question the ideal of bodily purity that must govern the practice of sports. From here comes the fear that the sport will collapse due to the collective inability to recognize "pure" athletes, especially when we consider that many non-athletes are profoundly "cyborgized" though artificial organs and parts, as well as through distinct types of medication.

On the other hand, experts in favor of the use of new technologies in sport question the arbitrary and binary methods that are at times used to define what constitutes a human being. Nevertheless, they do deny that technological advances necessarily dehumanize the practice of sport. Along these lines, they highlight that all individuals (and consequently all athletes, too) exercise freedom to question the limits imposed by nature, "to challenge the projected limited of modern sport, including those dealing with humans, machines and technology, and to explore new ways of being 'cyborg' though the interaction with technologies at our disposal" (Bostrom 2003b; 37). The continual efforts carried out by sport bureaucracy have also been denounced as they forcibly impose a rigid separation between "natural" and "technological" competitors.

Another strategy to demonstrate the inefficiency of excluding technologically modified athletes stems from highlighting the contradiction that this involves when compared to the current situation in which athletes have undergone therapeutic treatments that were unimaginable a number of years ago and without which they would not have achieved their actual level of success. In this way, for example, Messi—the now famous footballer—took growth hormones as an adolescent and Tiger Woods had eye surgery to overcome problems with short-sightedness. It is clear that these are cases of therapeutic treatments, but perhaps it will have to be considered that 1) there are already enhancement treatments (like vaccines); 2) as long as it is possible in the future that these initially therapeutic treatments allow patients to improve on previous abilities, or to broaden the spectrum of the human average, we will be on slippery ground. This boundary between therapeutic and enhancement treatments may become fuzzy. No single criterion exists to denote what is considered as a "disease," and consequently no limiting criterion is known for "therapies" either. For example, Borse offers a biological-determinist conception of disease, while Daniels advocates a social-constructivist focus. Depending on which criteria are adopted, (therapeutic) treatments can be more or less widespread. In other words, the scope of therapy could increase and in this way further broaden what qualifies as an enhancement treatment (Miah 2004).

The sports practiced by athletes who have had organs or mechanical parts implanted and their desire to take part in regular athletic competitions puts sport authorities in an ethical and legal tight spot. For example, an athlete who plays American football must be somewhat heavy to be able to successfully carry out his mission on the field, but this means reducing his life expectancy by an average of twenty-five years. Even if these negative health consequences, which improve athletic performance, are born out, the player is not barred from playing. An athlete who undergoes a "Tommy John"[3] operation could even play as pitcher for a baseball team. Nevertheless, another athlete who wants to replace an arm or a leg with an artificial one that would improve his or her scores in the field or allow him or her to play better would not be allowed to do so under current legislation. But what is the ethical difference between the two treatments? Take another example that could be perplexing if bans on devices that improved sport performance were banned ("any technical device that uses springs, wheels or any other element that provides the user with an advantage over other athletes who do not use such device" [Dvorsky 2007]). According to this ban, it would be prohibited that golfers use contact lenses to correct short-sightedness, but it would not be forbidden that they play after having surgery to correct the condition. This is the case of Tiger Woods. It would be both very odd and paradoxical to keep athletes from playing if they wore contacts, but allow them to play if they had undergone surgery when the results for all practical purposes are the same.

THE AESTHETIC PROBLEM

The fourth and final position is the problem with aesthetics, an objection of much shallower depth in theoretical and ethical terms. According to one response to this problem, the idea undergirding this critique is that spectators would have difficulty accepting sport competitions with "normal" athletes and those with atypical morphology, that is to say with cyborg athletes. Such difficulties could be based on feelings of aesthetic displeasure upon observing athletes with implants on the human body or simply because of inertia, i.e., it is difficult to get used to seeing a new kind of show.

In any case, this objection would not greatly affect the participation of those athletes in competition with normal athletes or in segregated competition, rather, it is directed at the fans' potential response. In other words, would spectators be willing to pay for tickets to see modified athletes in a stadium setting? Besides this question, there is another previous problem to be taken into account: the definition of what could be taken as atypical morphology. If what is taken as a point of reference is a significant variation compared to an established statistical norm, then exclusion could be extended to those athletes who are extremely tall or short. Titles or medals could even be revoked for those athletes with some type of physical anomaly that gave them an advantage over their rivals, as were the cases of Eero Mantyranta or Miguel Induráin. In addition, there are internal and external implants and prostheses. Why should the former be allowed and not the latter? Along these lines, an interesting case is the one of cyclist Floyd Landis who suffered a hip injury in 2003, resulting in a prosthetic hip in 2006. Curiously this did not generate problems even though the artificial hip could be clearly seen (Hilvoorde 2008; 22).

The second version of this critique is more powerful since it calls attention to the fact that the distinction must be drawn between modification and replacement of an organ. Following this line of reasoning, the surgical modification of a muscle, or even the modification of a cornea through laser surgery, would not be equal to implanting carbon fibres to replace biological legs.

This argument may fail under the first critique due to the fact that one type of technology is "not the same" as another. This argument has repercussions on the physical or external aspects of the athlete. If this were the meaning of the critique, the response is the same: it does not seem justifiable to exclude athletes with implants for aesthetic reasons. What is important is the athlete's ability, not the physical appearance.

> For, as well as overcoming considerable levels of prejudice and disadvantage due to his disability, Oscar Pistorius is as dedicated and trains as hard as any top athlete. The blades are mere means that make it possible for him to manifest his athletic prowess in his chosen events; they compensate for his lack of legs (Edwards 2008; 112).

But, "it is not the same" can have another meaning: the technology that replaces the organ in a body can have enhancement effects that are much greater than simple modification technologies may have. Two responses can be given with regard to this objection. It is not always the case that there is a direct or causal link between "replacement-greater performance" and "modification-decreased performance." For example, in the future, genetic interventions will likely produce substantial physiological improvements without simultaneously modifying the external appearance of the athlete. In addition, in paralympic trials, there are athletes with replacement prosthetics who have hardly any physical improvements, or, in any case, they are not comparable to the developments of "trained" athletes.

Yet another aspect to consider is that even if this link did exist, then the argument to establish regulatory changes to competition so that athletes could participate (or not) would impact performance in sport. Consequently, the eventual inequality would be seen irrespective of the type of technology that was produced or what the external physical appearance of the athlete looked like.

CONCLUSIONS

After examining in this chapter the three possible types of technological enhancements in sport (gene doping, implants and transhumans), I have considered which objections can be raised to technological enhancement. In this respect, I think that several aspects have to be taken into account: 1) the possibility of producing severe harm on athletes; 2) the effect it has on equality among athletes when the improvement grants an obvious advantage; 3) the dehumanization of sport; and 4) the aesthetic problem.

Regarding the first point, it is necessary to examine cases which would justify the eventual prohibition of enhancement treatments: 1) when there is harm to others; 2) when there is insufficient knowledge about the effects it would have on health. This happens, for example, in the case of gene doping, especially regarding the current state of research on germline treatments. However, for the case in which the health risk falls upon the athlete himself, the rest of the arguments that are used or that will be used to limit the participation of these new athletes are, as is currently the case with gene doping, clearly part and parcel of unjustified paternalism. A lift on the gene doping ban along with the establishment of external or independent medical testing procedures could provide more appropriate protection to athletes' health.

Regarding the second argument, it is necessary to distinguish between two possible effects of technological interventions: whether the improvement of physical ability is strictly "enhancing" or if it qualifies as "transhuman" in nature.

In terms of this distinction, which would require a degree of precision impossible to carry out within the scope of this chapter, if the interventions on the athlete are enhancements, the nature of the sport itself would not be violated. Therefore, moral reasons cannot be given to prohibit said treatments. Of course, to be able to accept such treatments, another condition is necessary: that equality of opportunity exists among athletes regarding access to improvements.

However, if the interventions are transhuman in nature, it seems obvious that sport would be substantially altered. The possibility that athletes with transhuman physical enhancements and untreated athletes could compete on the same playing field would affect equality among athletes, and in this way it would remove virtue completely from the results and take away the excitement of the game.

Nevertheless, the solution does not necessarily lie in banning such modifications, but rather it may eventually seem reasonable for transhuman athletes to establish separate competitions.

Regarding the third objection, which focuses on the dehumanization of sport, my point has been to highlight that the definition of "humanity" is far from peaceful, and that, in any case, if humanity is understood as a set of cognitive abilities that allow human agents to shape their future, then these enhancement techniques do not necessarily limit or eradicate these functions. This is so because athletes exercise their autonomy when they decide to opt for these treatments. In addition, I have shown that there is a lack of coherence in the argument for banning certain enhancement measures that are allowed in other areas of social life and within sports themselves.

Lastly, the aesthetic problem is nothing more than a perfectionist argument which has its core in a certain prejudice seen in the aesthetic preferences of the majority.

In short, my position has been to temper the "moral panic" that some may feel given the progressive (and future) use of technological enhancement treatments as used by athletes.

NOTES

1. When I speak of the genetic or natural lottery, I am referring to the phrase coined by John Rawls in his well-known book *A Theory of Justice* (Harvard: Belknap Press, 1971) which constitutes an argument for the principles of justice. He points out that many talents and abilities are the product of the "natural lottery" of inheritance. According to Rawls, no one can claim to deserve to have these genetic features and therefore no one can "deserve" to have a greater share of resources or benefits because of this "luck."

2. These features may be genetically determined, but they are influenced by an individual's relationship with the environment and by other circumstances linked to the subject's autonomous decision-making abilities.

3. "Tommy John surgery" is the media's name for the medical practice of ulnar collateral ligament (UCL) reconstruction of the elbow. It was in 1974 that Dr. Frank Jobe carried out an experiment on Tommy John, a pitcher for the Dodgers baseball team. Jobe extracted a tendon from John's right arm and used it to replace a severed one in the left arm. It was put into place with pins that opened in the bone above and below the elbow. The player was not only able to return to playing baseball, but he also won 170 more games in his career. In other words, his performance remarkably improved after the operation. See http://caibco.ucv.ve/caibco/vitae/VitaeOnce/Articulos/Traumatologia/paginashtml/Traumatologia.pdf).

Bibliography

Aguilera, A. *Estado y deporte*. Granada: ed. Comares, 1992.

Allison, L. "Sport and Nationalism." In *Handbook of Sport Studies*, edited by Eric Dunning and Jay Coakley. London: Sage, 2000.

Anderson, L. "Doctoring Risk: Responding to Risk-Taking in Athletes." In *The Ethics of Sports Medicine*, edited by C. Tamburrini and T. Tännsjö. London and New York: Routledge, 2009.

Atienza, M. and Ruiz Manero, J. *Ilícitos atípicos*. Madrid: Trotta, 2006.

Bairner, A. *Sport, Nationalism, and Globalization*. Albany: State University of New York, 2001.

Barón, D. A., Martin, D. M., Magd, S. A. "Dopaje en el deporte y su propagación a las poblaciones en riesgo: una revisión internacional." *World Psychiatry* 5, 2, 2007.

Bellioti, R. "Women, Sex and Sports." In *Philosophical Inquiry in Sport*, edited by Morgan, W. and Meier, K. Champaign, IL: Human Kinetics, 1995.

Bonde, H. "Masculine Movements: Sport and Masculinity in Denmark at the Turn of the Century." *Scandinavian Journal of History*, 21, 1996.

Bostrom, N. "Human Genetic Enhancements: A Transhumanist Perspective." *Journal of Value Inquiry*, 37, n.4 , 2003.

———. "Transhumanist Values." http://www.transhumanism.org/index.php/WTA/more/ transhumanist-values (Last accessed 5/23/06), (2003a).

Breivik, G. "Doping Games: A Game Theoretical Exploration of Doping." *International Review for Sociology of Sport* 27, 3, 1992.

———. "Against Chance: A Causal Theory of Winning in Sport." In *Values in Sport: Elitism, Nationalism, Gender Equality and the Scientific Manufacturing of Winners*, edited by T. Tännsjö and C. Tamburrini. London and New York: E&FN Spon (Routledge), 2000.

Brohm, J. M. *Sociología política del deporte*. México: FCE, 1982.

Butcher, R. and Schneider, A. "Fair Play as Respect for the Game." In *Ethics in Sport* edited by Morgan, W., Meier, K. V. and Schneider, A. Champaign, IL: Human Kinetics, 2001.

Butryn. T. D. "Posthuman Podiums: Cyborg Narrative of Elite Track and Field Athletes." *Sociology of Sport Journal* 20, 2003.

Cagigal, J. M. *Deporte y agresió*. Madrid: Alianza Deporte, 1990.

Camporesi, S. "Oscar Pistorius, Enhancement and Post-Humans." *Journal of Medical Ethics* 34, 2008.

Cazorla Prieto, L. M. *Deporte y Estado*. Madrid: Politeia, 1979.

Cultberson, L. "Genetic Enhancement in the Dark." *Journal of Philosophy of Sport* 36, 2, 2009.

D'Agostino, F. "The Ethos of Games." In *Philosophical Inquiry in Sport*, edited by Morgan W.and Meier, K., Champaign, IL: Human Kinetics, 1995.

De Miguel, I. "Quimeras e híbridos: ¿Problema ético o problema para la ética?." *Dilemata*, 6, 2011.

Dixon, N. "A Justification of Moderate Patriotism in Sport" In *Values in Sport: Elitism, Nationalism, Gender Equality, and the Scientific Manufacturing of Winners* edited by T. Tännsjö and C. Tamburrini. London and New York: E&FN Spon (Routledge), 2000.

———. "On Winning and Athletic Superiority." In *Sports Ethics: An Anthology* edited by Jan Boxill, Malden-Oxford; Blackwell, 2003.

————. "Boxing, Paternalism and Legal Moralism." In *Ethics in Sport*, edited by W. J. Morgan, Champaign, IL: Human Kinetics, 2007.

————. "The Ethics of Supporting Sport Teams." In *Ethics in Sport*, edited by W. J. Morgan, Champaign, IL: Human Kinetics, 2007.

Douglas, Th. "Enhancement in Sport, and Enhancement Outside Sport." *Studies in Ethics, Law, and Technology* 1, 1, 2007.

Durán, J. *El vandalismo en el fútbol*. Madrid: Gymnos, 1996.

Dvorsky G. "Is the world ready for cyborg athletes?" 25 April 2007. http://ieet.org/index.php/IEET/more/dvorsky20070425 (accessed 14 July 2008).

Dworkin S. H. and Messner, M. A. "Just Do . . . What? Sport, Bodies, Gender" in *Gender and Sport: A Reader*, edited by S. Scraton and A. Flintoff. London and New York: Routledge, 2002.

Dworkin, R. *Taking Rights Seriously*. London: Duckworth, 1978.

Elias, N. and Dunning, E. *Deporte y ocio en el proceso de civilización*. México: F.C.E., 1992.

English, J. "Sex Equality in Sports." In *Philosophical Inquiry in Sport*, edited by Morgan, W. and Meier, K. Champaign, IL: Human Kinetics, 1995.

Feinberg, W. "Nationalism in a Comparative Mode: A Response to Charles Taylor." In *The Morality of Nationalism* edited by McKim, R. and McMahan, Oxford and New York: Oxford University Press, 1997.

Fraleigh, W. O. "Intentional Rules Violations-One More Time." In *Ethics in Sport*, edited by W. J. Morgan. Champaign, IL: Human Kinetics, 2007.

Fukuyama, F. *Our Posthuman Future: Consequences of the Biotechnology Revolution*. London: Profile Books, 2002.

Gamero, E. "Violencia en el deporte y violencia en espectáculos deportivos: referencia histórica y problemática actual." In *Régimen jurídico de la violencia en deporte* edited by Millán Garrido, A. Barcelona: ed. Bosch, 2006.

Gomberg, P. "Patriotism in Sports and in War." In *Values in Sport: Elitism, Nationalism, Gender Equality, and the Scientific Manufacturing of Winners* edited by T. Tännsjö and C. Tamburrini. London and New York: E&FN Spon (Routledge), 2000.

Gómez, A. "La violencia en el deporte. Un análisis desde la psicología social." *Revista de Psicología Social* 22, 1, 2007.

Gracia Marco, L., Rey López, J. P., Casajús Mallén, J. A. "El dopaje en los Juegos Olímpicos de verano (1968–2008)" Apunts: Medicina de l'esport. 44, 162, 2009.

Haugen, K. K. "The Performance-Enhancing Drug Game." *Journal of Sports Economics* 5, 1, 2004.

Hoberman, J. *Mortal Engines: The Science of Performance and the Dehumanization of Sport*. New York: The Free Press, 1992.

Huizinga, J. *Homo Ludens*, London: Roy Publishers, 1995

Kayser, B., Mauron A. and Miah, A. "Current Anti-Doping Policy: A Critical Appraisal." *BMC Medical Ethics* 8, 2, 2005.

King, A. "Nationalism and Sport." In *The Handbook of Nations and Nationalism*, edited by Delanty, G. and Kumar, K., London and New Delhi:Sage, 2006.

Leach, R. E. "Violence and Sport." In *Sport Ethics: An Anthology* edited by Boxill, Jan. Malden-Oxford-Victoria: Blackwell Pub., 2003.

Leaman,O. "Cheating and Fair Play in Sport." In *Philosophic Inquiry in Sport*, eds. W.J. Morgan and K.V. Meier. 2nd ed. Champaign, IL: Human Kinetics, 2001.

Loland, S. and McNamee, M. "Fair Play and the Ethos of Sport: An Eclectic Philosophical Framework." *Journal of Philosophy of Sport*, 27, 2000.

Loland, S. "The Ethics of Performance-Enhancing Technology in Sport." *Journal of the Philosophy of Sport*, 36, 157, 2009.

————. *Fair Play in Sport: A Moral Norm System*. London and New York: Routledge, 2002.

Longman J. "An Amputee Sprinter: Is He Disabled or Too-Abled?" *New York Times* May 15, 2007.

López Frías, F. J. "Reivindicando una ética del deporte como filosofía aplicada: El deporte como cuestión moral." *Dilemata* 2, 2010.

MacIntyre, A. *After Virtue*. Notre Dame: Bloomsbury Academic and University of Notre Dame Press, 1981.

———. "Is Patriotism a Virtue?" *Lindley Lecture*. Kansas: University of Kansas, 1984.

Margalit, A. "The Moral Psychology of Nationalism." In *The Morality of Nationalism* edited by McKim, R. and McMahan, Oxford and New York: Oxford University Press, 1997.

McFee, G. *Sport, Rules, and Values*. London and New York: Routledge, 2004

McMahan, J. "The Limits of National Partiality." In *The Morality of Nationalism* edited by McKim, R. and McMahan, Oxford and New York: Oxford University Press, 1997.

McNamee, M. "Sporting Practices, Institutions, and Virtues; A Critique and a Restate-ment." *Journal of the Philosophy of Sport* 22, 1995.

McNamee, M. and Edwards, S. S. "Medical Technology and Slippery Slopes." *Journal of Medical Ethics* 32, 9, 2006.

Messner, M. "Sports and Male Domination: The Female Athlete as Contested Ideological Terrain." In *Philosophical Inquiry in Sport*, edited by Morgan W. and Meier, K. Champaign, IL: Human Kinetics, 1995.

Miah, A. *Genetically Modified Athletes*, London and New York: E&FN Spon (Routledge), 2004.

Millán Garrido, A. (ed). *Régimen jurídico de la violencia en deporte*. Barcelona: ed. Bosch, 2006.

Moller, V. *The Ethics of Doping and Anti-Doping*. London and New York: Routledge, 2010.

Morgan W. J. *Ethics in Sport*. Champaign, IL: Human Kinetics, 2007.

———. "Sports and the Moral Discourse of Nations." In *Values in Sport: Elitism, Nationalism, Gender Equality, and the Scientific Manufacturing of Winners*, edited by T. Tännsjö and C. Tamburrini. London and New York: E&FN Spon (Routledge), 2000.

Morgan W. J., Meier, K. *Philosophical Inquiry in Sport*. Champaign, IL: Human Kinetics, 1995.

Morgan W. J., Meir, K. and Schneider, A. *Ethics in Sport*. Champaign, IL: Human Kinetics, 2001.

Munthe, Ch. "Selected Champions: Making Winners in the Age of Genetic Technology." In *Values in Sport: Elitism, Nationalism, Gender Equality, and the Scientific Manufacturing of Winners*, edited by T. Tännsjö and C. Tamburrini. London and New York: E&FN Spon (Routledge), 2000.

Murray T. *"From Birth to Death and Bench to Clinic"*: *The Hastings Center Bioethics Briefing Book for Journalists, Policymakers and Campaigns*. Garrison: The Hastings Center, 2008.

Navas Renedo, B. "Las reglas del juego como límite a la intervención del Derecho Penal." In *Régimen jurídico de la violencia en deporte*, edited by Millán Garrido, A. Barcelona: ed. Bosch, 2006.

Oliver, K. "Enhancing Evolution Whose Body? Whose Choice?" *The Southern Journal of Philosophy* 48, 2010.

Parry. J. "Violence and Aggression in Contemporary Sport." In *Ethics and Sport*, edited by McNamee, M. and Parry, J. London and New York: E & FN Spon (Routledge), 1998.

Payero López, L. "La nación se la juega; relaciones entre el nacionalismo y el deporte en España." *Ágora para la EF y el Deporte* 10, 2009.

Postow, B. C. "Women and Masculine Sports." In *Philosophical Inquiry in Sport*, edited by Morgan W. and Meier, K. Champaign, IL: Human Kinetics, 1995.

Puig, N. and Mosquera, M. J. "Género y edad en el deporte." In *Sociología del deporte* edited by M. García Ferrando, N. Puig, and F. Lagardera, Alianza: Madrid, 1998.

Ramos Gordillo, A. S: "Lucha contra el dopaje como objetivo de salud." *Adicciones* 11, 4, 1999.

Reguera, G. "La identidad de los clubes de fútbol." In *Culturas del fútbol*, edited by Solar L. and Reguera, G. Vitoria-Gasteiz: Bassarai, 2008.

Ríos Corbacho, J. M. "Una aproximación a la lesiones deportivas en el ámbito del Derecho Penal." *Revista de Derecho Penal* 1, 2010.

Russell, J. S. "Are Rules All an Umpire Has to Work With?" *Journal of the Philosophy of Sport* 26, 1999.

Sandel, M. *The Case Against Perfection: Ethics in the Age of Genetic Engineering*, Cambridge, MA, and London: The Belknap Press, 2007.

Savulescu, J. "Genetically Modified Animals: Should There Be Limits to Engineering the Animal Kingdom?" In *The Oxford Handbook of Animal Ethics* edited by Beauchamp T. and Frey R. G. Oxford: Oxford University Press, 2011.

Savulescu, J., Foddy, B. and Clayton, M. "Why We Should Allow Performance Enhancing Drugs in Sport." *British Journal of Sports and Medicine* 38, 2004.

Schneider A. and Rupert, J. "Constructing Winners: The Science and Ethics of Genetically Manipulating Athletes." *Journal of Philosophy of Sport*, 2009.

Schneider, A. "On the Definition of 'Woman' in the Sport Context." In *Values in Sport: Elitism, Nationalism, Gender Equality, and the Scientific Manufacturing of Winners*, edited by T. Tännsjö and C. Tamburrini. London and New York: E&FN Spon (Routledge), 2000.

Schneider, A. and Butcher, R.: "Ethics, Sport, and Boxing" In *Ethics in Sport*, edited by W. J. Morgan, K. V. Meier and A. Schneider. Champaign, IL: Human Kinetics, 2001.

———. "A philosophical overview of the argument on banning doping in sport." In *Values in Sport: Elitism, Nationalism, Gender Equality, and the Scientific Manufacturing of Winners*, edited by T. Tännsjö and C. Tamburrini. London and New York: E&FN Spon (Routledge), 2000.

Schneider, R. *Ethics of Sport and Athletics*. Baltimore: Wolters Kluwer, 2009.

Scraton, S. and Flintoff, A. eds. *Gender and Sport: A Reader*, London and New York: Routledge, 2002.

Simon, R. "Good Competition and Drug Enhanced Performance." In *Philosophical Inquiry in Sport*, edited by Morgan, W. and Meier, K. Champaign, IL: Human Kinetics, 1995.

———. "Gender, Equity and Inequity in Athletics." In *Philosophical Inquiry in Sport*, edited by Morgan W. and Meier, K. Champaign, IL: Human Kinetics, 2000.

———. *Fair Play. Sports, Values, and Society*. Boulder-San Francisco-Oxford: Westview Press, 1991.

———. "The Ethics of Strategic Fouling." In *Ethics in Sport*, edited by W. J. Morgan, Champaign, IL: Human Kinetics, 2007.

Skirstad, B. "Gender Verification in Competitive Sport: Turning from Research to Action." In *Values in Sport: Elitism, Nationalism, Gender Equality, and the Scientific Manufacturing of Winners*, edited by T. Tännsjö and C. Tamburrini. London and New York: E&FN Spon (Routledge), 2000.

Smith, M. "What Is Sport Violence? In *Sport Ethics: An Anthology*, edited by Boxill, Jan. Malden-Oxford-Victoria: Blackwell Pub., 2003.

Suits, B. "The Elements of Sport." In *Philosophical Inquiry in Sport*, edited by Morgan, W. and Meier, K. Champaign, IL: Human Kinetics, 1995.

———. *The Grasshopper: Games, Life, and Utopia*. Toronto: University of Toronto Press, 1978.

Tamburrini, C. *¿La mano de Dios? Una visión distinta del deporte*. Buenos Aires: Eds. Continente, 2000.

———. "What's Wrong with Doping?" In *Values in Sport: Elitism, Nationalism, Gender Equality, and the Scientific Manufacturing of Winners*, edited by T. Tännsjö and C. Tamburrini. London and New York: E&FN Spon (Routledge), 2000.

Tännsjö, T. "Against Sexual Discrimination in Sports." In *Ethics in Sport*, edited by W. J. Morgan, Champaign, IL: Human Kinetics, 2007.

———. "Is our admiration for Sports Heroes Fascistoid?" In *Ethics in Sport*, edited by W. J. Morgan, Champaign, IL: Human Kinetics, 2007.

———. "Medical Enhancement and the Ethos of Elite Sport." In *Human Enhancement*, edited by Savulescu, J. and Bostrom, N. Oxford: Oxford University Press, 2009.

Tännsjö, T. and Tamburrini, C. *Values in Sport: Elitism, Nationalism, Gender Equality, and the Scientific Manufacturing of Winners*. London and New York: E&FN Spon (Routledge), 2000.

——. "Las bioamazonas del fútbol." In *¿La pelota no dobla? Ensayos filosóficos en torno al fútbol*, edited by Torres, C. and Campos, D. Buenos Aires: Ed. Zorzal, 2006.

——. *The Ethics of Sport Medicine*. London and New York: Routledge, 2009.

Taylor, Ch. "Nationalism and Modernity." In *The Morality of Nationalism*, edited by McKim, R. and McMahan, Oxford and New York: Oxford University Press, 1997.

Todd, T. "Anabolic Steroids: The Gremlins of Sport." *Journal of Sport History* 14, 1, 1987.

Torres, C. "What Counts as Part of a Game? A Look at Skills." *Journal of the Philosophy of Sport* 27, 2000.

Verroken, M. "Drug Use and Abuse in Sport." In *Drugs in Sport*, edited by D. R. Mottram, 29–63. London: Routledge, 2005.

Wenz, P. "Human Equality in Sports." In *Philosophical Inquiry in Sport*, edited by Morgan, W. and Meier, K. Champaign, IL: Human Kinetics, 1995.

Wolbring, G. "Hearing Beyond the Normal Enabled by Therapeutic Devices: The Role of the Recipient and the Hearing Profession." *Neuroethics*, 2011

——. "Who Will Be the Future Olympic and Paralympic Athlete: Advances in Science and Technology, Bodily Assistive Devices, and the Future Face and Purpose of Sport." http://www.bioethicsanddisability.org/vancouverpodcast.html (last visited: 2/10/2011) 2011b.

Wonkam, A., Fieggen, K. and Ramesar R. "Beyond the Caster Semenya Controversy: The Case of the Use of Genetics for Gender Testing in Sport." *Journal of Genetic Counsel* 19, 2010.

Young, I. M. "The Exclusion of Women from Sport: Conceptual and Existential Dimensions." In *Philosophical Inquiry in Sport*, edited by Morgan, W. and Meier, K. Champaign, IL: Human Kinetics, 1995.

Zettler, P. J. "Is It Cheating to Use Cheetahs?: The Implications of Technologically Innovative Prostheses for Sports Values and Rules." *Boston University International Law Journal* 27, 2009.

Index